P9-DXO-262

marie claire

flavours

thank you

Thank you yet again to my publisher, Catie Ziller, for letting me do what I do best and believing in my books, and to Matt Handbury and Paul Dykzeul for looking after 'Donna Hay'. Petrina Tinslay survives yet another book in style—thank you for the beautiful photography and for keeping me on my toes. Vanessa Holden, my friend who keeps me in line, and the most stylish art director a girl could wish for. Her new baby grew as fast as the book did. Thank you, new baby, for staying put until the book was finished—I just can't wait to meet you. Briget Palmer and Ben Masters, the best kitchen team in town. Thank you for your stamina, patience, sense of humour, perfectionism and devotion to the book. Jo-Pattie ('Oh my goodness, this is fantastic! Oooh, it's my new favourite; what is it?')—thanks for the encouragement and support. Susan Gray, my thorough and easygoing editor, who made the workings of the book so easy. Billy Wilson, my partner, who props me up when the going gets tough and picks me up when I fall over. Tony Lee at Omega Smeg—how happy you make me feel every morning when I open the door to the studio and see my fantastic Smeg kitchen. My mum, dad, sisters, nieces and friends who support me and make me feel good. Thanks also to Simon, Angela, Sarah J., Jody Vassallo, Alice and Bob.

Thank you to the Antico family for the supply of perfect fruits and vegetables; Con, James and Cathy at Demcos for the freshest seafoods; all the butchers at Paddington Fresh; Shelly at Mud Australia for her irresistible fine matt ceramics. Brian at Bison Homewares for the fantastic fresh-coloured ceramics. Toby at Toby's Estate Coffee for keeping me fuelled up on the finest caffeine around.

Many thanks for the props and equipment supplied by: Francalia (Limoges); Boda Nova; Orrefors Kosta Boda; Empire Homewares; The Bay Tree; Riedel; Country Road Homewares; Dinosaur Designs; Orson & Blake; Witchery; Wheel & Barrow; Hale Imports (Pillivuyt); Strutt Linen; Breville; Phillips.

Published by Murdoch Books®. First published 2000.

Art Director/Designer: Vanessa Holden
Author and Stylist: Donna Hay
Photographer: Petrina Tinslay
Project Manager: Anna Waddington
Editor: Susan Gray

Group CEO and Publisher: Anne Wilson
Group General Manager: Mark Smith
Associate Publisher: Catie Ziller
Production Manager: Liz Fitzgerald

National Library of Australia Cataloguing-in-Publication Data
Hay, Donna.
Flavours.
Includes index.
ISBN 0 86411 992 5.
1. Cookery. I. Tinslay, Petrina. II. Title. III. Title: marie claire.
641.5

Text © Donna Hay 2000. Photography © Petrina Tinslay 2000. Design © Murdoch Books® 2000.

Murdoch Books®, GPO Box 1203, Sydney, NSW Australia 1045.
Distributed in Australia by Gordon and Gotch Ltd, 68 Kingsgrove Road, Belmore, NSW 2182.
Distributed in NZ by Golden Press, a division of HarperCollins Publishers, 31 View Road, Glenfield, PO Box 1, Auckland 1.

Printed by Toppan Printing Hong Kong Co. Ltd. PRINTED IN CHINA. First printed 2000.

All rights reserved. No part of this publication may be reproduced, stored in any retrieval system or transmitted in any form or by any means, electronic, mechanical, photocopying, recording or otherwise, without the prior written permission of the publisher. Murdoch Books® is a trademark of Murdoch Magazines Pty Ltd.

marie claire

flavours

donna hay

photography by
petrina tinslay

MURDOCH BOOKS®
Sydney • London • Vancouver • New York

contents

introduction

From the tempting mellow smoothness of vanilla to the refreshing tangy bite of citrus, the seductive sweetness of chocolate to the fiery punch of chilli, simple and essential flavours can, when combined imaginatively with other ingredients, provide sensory experiences that not only stimulate the tastebuds but tantalise the mind.

marie claire flavours is an intoxicating journey through some of our favourite flavours. Exciting the palate with a diverse range of tastes, from sweet through to sour, from piquant to punchy, each chapter invites you to enliven your senses by exploring the origins of various aromatic ingredients, using them first in a range of simple, good ideas and then showcasing the flavours in a range of mouthwatering recipes.

As always, the *marie claire* philosophy is to start with good-quality produce, using fresh ingredients to complement and contrast with your base flavour in order to create the perfect taste experience.

More information about ingredients and basic recipes marked with a star* can be found in the glossary.

vanilla

basics

Vanilla is the flavour derived from cured beans or seed pods of a climbing vine of a family of tropical orchids. Native to Central America, the vanilla orchid was discovered by European traders in the 16th century but was for many years shrouded in mystery: no-one could get the orchid to produce its seed pods away from its native lands. It was later discovered that the orchid could only be naturally pollinated by the native melipone bee and hummingbird, neither of which existed in the new growing areas or countries.

The orchid flowers for less than one day. In commercial operations today, each individual flower is pollinated by hand. After pollination, the plump yellow pod takes four weeks to develop. The pod is then harvested and the curing or fermenting process begins. The mature pods are first steamed and then slowly dried in order to develop and mature the vanillin flavour in the pod. The oxidisation of the pods during this process causes them to brown and develop their characteristic smooth, tobacco-like aroma.

vanilla seeds

It is in the seeds that much of the deep vanilla flavour of the bean is located. Split a whole vanilla bean and scrape down the length of the inside to remove these tiny black specks. Add both the seeds and the bean in recipes that ask for a split and scraped vanilla bean.

vanilla beans

These are the dried, fermented pods of the vanilla orchid. The cured pods or beans should be pliable, moist and plumpish. The beans can be used whole, or split to release the flavoured seeds. They should be stored in an airtight container and can be reused when washed and dried, although they will lose a little of their strength each time they are used.

vanilla sugar

Vanilla sugar is sugar that has been perfumed with vanilla beans. It is sometimes used in baking as a mild flavouring. The sugar is also great over breakfast cereal, porridge or in coffee. Imitations of this product are available, so read the package before purchasing to ensure you're getting the true thing. Vanilla sugar can be flavoured by infusing the whole beans in the sugar, or by placing the sugar and beans together in a food processor, then sieving to remove large pieces of the outer bean. (See page 187 for easy instructions.)

vanilla essence

This is inferior in quality to vanilla extract and is sometimes chemically synthesised from the essential oil of cloves, the lignin in wood wastes, or coal-tar extracts. For a true and unmistakable vanilla taste and perfume, use only vanilla beans or vanilla extract.

vanilla extract

This is a hydroalcoholic solution that contains the extracted flavour and aroma of the vanilla bean. Pure vanilla extract is labelled as such and has a rich perfume, a deep amber colour and a syrupy consistency. If vanilla beans are unavailable, then vanilla extract is the best substitute. Substitute 1 teaspoon or more of vanilla extract for 1 vanilla bean in a recipe. Store the extract in a dark place.

vanilla essence

vanilla beans

vanilla seeds

vanilla extract

vanilla sugar

good ideas

vanilla coffee

Finely chop vanilla beans and blend them with medium-ground plunger coffee. Next time you plunge your coffee it will have a mellow vanilla aroma and flavour to it.

vanilla scent

Wrap vanilla beans in tissue paper or glassine envelopes and place in your kitchen cupboards or refrigerator for a rich, mellow vanilla scent.

vanilla tea

Mix finely chopped vanilla beans with a quality black leaf tea. Seal and store in a cool, dry place for 2 weeks before brewing in a pot for a vanilla-scented tea.

warm milk

For pure liquid relaxation, warm some milk in a saucepan over low heat, flavour with a little sugar and vanilla extract, and add malted milk powder for extra comfort.

vanilla mascarpone

Stir 250g (8 oz) of mascarpone* with ¼ cup (2 fl oz) of cream and 1 teaspoon of vanilla extract. Add sieved icing (confectioners') sugar to taste. Use this mixture to fill tart shells, serve with sliced fresh fruits, or use instead of thick cream with desserts.

vanilla syrup

Place a split vanilla bean in a saucepan with 1 cup of sugar and 1½ cups (12 fl oz) of water. Stir over low heat until the sugar has dissolved, then simmer until well flavoured. Add to milk for a true vanilla milkshake, or pour over ice cream or warm breakfast porridge. Store in the refrigerator.

vanilla maple syrup

Heat 300ml (10 fl oz) of pure maple syrup and 2 split vanilla beans in a saucepan. Simmer gently for a few minutes or until the maple syrup is fragrant. Store in the refrigerator and serve over yoghurt, fruit or pancakes.

vanilla peach trifle

vanilla snap biscuits

vanilla-soaked fruits

vanilla peach trifle

1 cup (8 fl oz) sweet dessert wine—sauternes or
   botrytis riesling
1½ cups sugar
1 vanilla bean, split and scraped
2 peaches, thickly sliced
1 small sponge cake* or 16 sponge biscuits
vanilla cream
300g (10 oz) thick mascarpone*
¾ cup (6 fl oz) cream
3 tablespoons icing (confectioners') sugar, sieved
1 teaspoon vanilla extract

Place the dessert wine, sugar and vanilla bean in a frying
pan over medium–high heat and stir to dissolve the sugar.
Simmer for 2 minutes. Add the peach slices and cook for
1 minute each side. Remove from the pan and set aside.
To make the vanilla cream, place the mascarpone, cream,
icing sugar and vanilla in a bowl and mix to combine.
To serve, place a slice of sponge on each of 6 serving
plates. Drizzle with some of the pan juices from the
peaches, then top with a few spoonfuls of vanilla cream.
Top with the peaches and the remaining pan sauce.
Serve immediately. Serves 6.

vanilla snap biscuits

185g (6 oz) butter, chopped
1 cup caster (superfine) sugar
2 teaspoons vanilla extract
2½ cups plain (all-purpose) flour
1 egg

Place the butter, sugar and vanilla extract in a food
processor and process until smooth. Add the flour and
egg and process until combined. Remove the mixture
from the food processor and wrap in plastic wrap.
Refrigerate the dough for 30 minutes or until firm.
Preheat the oven to 180°C (350°F). Roll out the dough
on non-stick baking paper or a lightly floured surface until
5mm (¼ inch) thick. Cut out the dough, using a 7cm
(2¾ inch) round cookie cutter, and place the biscuits on
baking trays lined with non-stick baking paper. Bake for
10–13 minutes or until the biscuits are golden on the
bases. Cool on the trays. Serve with coffee or tea or as
a crisp biscuit with dessert. Makes 24.

vanilla-soaked fruits

1 cup sugar
2 cups (16 fl oz) water
1 vanilla bean, split and scraped
4 mixed halved and seeded fruit, such as apricots, peaches,
   nectarines, small sweet apples, pears or plums

Place the sugar, water and vanilla bean in a saucepan
and stir over low heat until the sugar has dissolved.
Add the fruit and poach gently over low heat for
5 minutes or until the fruits are soft.
Serve warm in deep bowls with the syrup and thick
cream or ice cream. Serves 4.

vanilla meringues

4 egg whites
1¼ cups caster (superfine) sugar
1 tablespoon cornflour (cornstarch)
1 teaspoon white vinegar
1 teaspoon vanilla extract
seeds from 1 vanilla bean, optional

Preheat the oven to 130°C (260°F). Place the egg whites
in the bowl of an electric mixer and beat until soft peaks
form. Add the sugar a little at a time, beating well as you
add it. Sift the cornflour over the mixture and fold through
with the vinegar, vanilla extract and vanilla seeds.
Take half of the mixture, shape into six small rounds and
place on a baking tray lined with non-stick baking paper.
Repeat with the remaining mixture, placing the meringues
on a separate baking tray. Place both trays in the oven and
reduce the heat to 100°C (200°F). Cook for 30–35 minutes.
Turn the oven off and allow the meringues to cool in the
oven. Serve with strong coffee or with fresh fruits and
cream. Makes 12 meringues.

vanilla meringues

vanilla plum tart

vanilla truffles

vanilla cream cakes

vanilla

vanilla plum tart

1 quantity sweet shortcrust pastry* or 375g (12 oz)
   ready-prepared pastry
filling
45g (1½ oz) butter
1 cup caster (superfine) sugar
1¼ cups almond meal (ground almonds)
1 teaspoon vanilla extract
¼ cup plain (all-purpose) flour
2 eggs
4 plums, thickly sliced

Preheat the oven to 200°C (400°F). Roll out the pastry on
a lightly floured surface until 3mm (⅛ inch) thick. Place
the pastry into a 26cm (10½ inch) removable-base tart tin
and prick the base and side with a fork. Line the pastry
with non-stick baking paper and fill with rice or baking
weights. Bake for 6 minutes, remove the baking weights
and paper and bake for a further 6 minutes or until golden.
Reduce the oven to 180°C (350°F).
To make the filling, place the butter, sugar, almonds, vanilla
extract, flour and eggs in a food processor and process
until smooth. Spread over the tart base. Press the plum
slices over the almond mixture and bake for 30–40 minutes
or until the filling is golden and the fruit is soft.
Serve in wedges with vanilla ice cream. Serves 8.

vanilla truffles

500g (1 lb) white chocolate, chopped
2 tablespoons water
180g (6 oz) butter, chopped
2 teaspoons vanilla extract
seeds from 1 vanilla bean
icing (confectioners') sugar

Line the base and sides of an 18cm (7 inch) square cake
tin with non-stick baking paper.
Place the chocolate, water and butter in a saucepan
over low heat and stir gently until the chocolate has
melted. Continue stirring over the heat for 10 minutes.
Remove from the heat and stir through the vanilla extract
and vanilla seeds. Pour into the cake tin and refrigerate
for 2 hours or until set. Remove from the tin and cut into
small squares.
To serve, sift icing sugar onto a plate and press both sides
of each chocolate square into the icing sugar, leaving the
sides uncoated. Serve with coffee. Makes 16.

vanilla cream cakes

185g (6 oz) butter
¾ cup caster (superfine) sugar
1 teaspoon vanilla extract
3 eggs
1½ cups plain (all-purpose) flour
1½ teaspoons baking powder
vanilla cream
1¼ cups (10 fl oz) thick cream (48% butter fat)
1 teaspoon vanilla extract

Preheat the oven to 160°C (315°F). Place the butter, sugar
and vanilla extract in the bowl of an electric mixer and beat
until light and creamy. Add the eggs and beat well.
Sift the flour and baking powder over the mixture and fold
to combine. Spoon the mixture into twelve ½-cup (4 fl oz)
capacity non-stick muffin tins. Bake for 20 minutes or until
the cakes are cooked when tested with a skewer. Cool in
the tins for 4 minutes, then cool on wire racks.
To make the vanilla cream, place the cream and vanilla
extract in a bowl and whisk until thick. To serve, cut the
cakes in half and spread with half the vanilla cream.
Spread the remaining vanilla cream over the tops of the
cakes and serve. Makes 12 small cakes.

vanilla and saffron pears

8 small pears, peeled
4 cups (32 fl oz) water
1½ cups sugar
1 vanilla bean, split and scraped
pinch saffron threads*
1 slice ginger
1 small piece lemon rind

Place the pears, water, sugar, vanilla bean, saffron, ginger
and lemon rind in a saucepan. Cook over low heat for
30 minutes or until the pears are just soft, turning them
occasionally. Serve in bowls with the vanilla and saffron
poaching liquid. Serves 4.

20

vanilla and saffron pears

steamed vanilla blood plum puddings

4 tablespoons maple syrup
4 blood plums, thickly sliced
puddings
2 cups self-raising (self-rising) flour
1/2 teaspoon baking powder
90g (3 oz) butter
1 teaspoon vanilla extract
2 eggs
2/3 cup demerara sugar*
3/4 cup (6 fl oz) milk

Place 2 teaspoons of maple syrup in the base of each of six 1-cup (8 fl oz) capacity ovenproof bowls. Arrange the plum slices on top of the syrup.
To make the puddings, place the flour, baking powder, butter, vanilla extract, eggs, sugar and milk in a food processor and process until smooth. Spoon over the plums. Cover the puddings with a circle of baking paper and then cover with aluminium foil and secure with string. Place in one or two large saucepans of simmering water. The water should come halfway up the sides of the bowls. Cover and cook for 1 hour or until the puddings are firm. Serves 6.
note – You may need to top up the saucepans with more boiling water while cooking the puddings.

vanilla milk gelato

2 cups (16 fl oz) milk
1 vanilla bean, split and scraped
4 egg yolks
3/4 cup sugar
1 cup (8 fl oz) cream

Place the milk and the vanilla bean in a saucepan over medium heat and heat until almost boiling. Beat together the egg yolks and sugar. Remove the milk from the heat and whisk through the egg mixture. Return to the heat and stir for 3–4 minutes or until the mixture thickens slightly. Remove from the heat and discard the vanilla bean. Add the cream and allow to cool.
Pour the mixture into an ice cream maker and follow the manufacturer's instructions until the gelato is frozen and scoopable. Alternatively, place the mixture in a metal container and freeze, beating at 1-hour intervals, until the gelato is scoopable.
Serve with vanilla snap biscuits or in cups as a sweet, cool snack or dessert. Serves 4–6.
note – For a more intense vanilla flavour, add a teaspoon or two of vanilla extract to the milk.

vanilla school pastries

375g (12 oz) ready-prepared puff pastry
icing (confectioners') sugar, for dusting
vanilla pastry cream
1 1/2 cups (12 fl oz) milk
1 cup (8 fl oz) cream
2 teaspoons vanilla extract
2/3 cup sugar
1/3 cup cornflour (cornstarch)
1/2 cup (4 fl oz) water
6 egg yolks

Preheat the oven to 180°C (350°F). Roll out the pastry on a lightly floured surface until 3mm (1/8 inch) thick. Cut the pastry into two 15 x 25cm (6 x 10 inch) rectangles. Place on a baking tray lined with non-stick baking paper, top with another baking tray as a weight, and bake for 15 minutes or until puffed and golden. Allow to cool on racks.
To make the pastry cream, place the milk, cream, vanilla extract and sugar in a saucepan over medium–low heat and heat until hot but not boiling. Mix the cornflour and water to a smooth paste and then whisk into the hot milk mixture. Add the egg yolks and whisk, simmering for 6 minutes or until the mixture has thickened and the cornflour has cooked through.
Allow the mixture to cool in the saucepan to room temperature without refrigerating. Spread one of the baked pastry sheets with the vanilla pastry cream and top with the remaining pastry sheet. Refrigerate for at least 1 hour to set. Sprinkle with icing sugar and cut into pieces to serve. Makes 12 pieces.

vanilla and rhubarb jam

1kg (2 lb) finely chopped rhubarb
3 green apples, peeled, cored and finely chopped
1 vanilla bean, split and scraped
1/2 cup (4 fl oz) water
3 tablespoons lemon juice
800g (1 lb 10 oz) sugar

Place the rhubarb, apple, vanilla bean and water in a large saucepan over medium heat. Cover and cook for 5 minutes or until the rhubarb is soft.
Add the lemon juice and sugar and simmer uncovered for 45–60 minutes or until the mixture is thick. While the jam is still cooking, remove the foam from the surface with a large metal spoon.
To test to see if the jam is set, place a small spoonful on a well-chilled plate. It should immediately thicken. Store in sterilised jars* and serve on buttered toast or pancakes. Makes 4 cups.

steamed vanilla blood plum puddings

vanilla school pastries

vanilla milk gelato

vanilla and rhubarb jam

vanilla risotto

caramelised vanilla orange

green apple and vanilla snow

vanilla risotto

3¼ cups (26 fl oz) milk
1 vanilla bean, split and scraped
2 tablespoons butter
1 cup arborio* or risotto rice
¼ cup sugar
¼ cup (2 fl oz) cream
¼ cup (2 fl oz) milk, extra

Place the milk and vanilla bean in a saucepan over medium heat and heat for 5 minutes or until hot but not boiling. Melt the butter in a separate saucepan over medium heat and add the rice. Cook, stirring, for 3 minutes or until the rice becomes translucent.
Add the hot milk a cup at a time, stirring between additions until the liquid has been absorbed and the rice is al dente. Stir through the sugar, cream and extra milk. Allow to stand for 2 minutes, then spoon into bowls to serve.
Serve with small bowls of simmered winter fruits such as quince, rhubarb, apple or pear for dessert, or sprinkle with brown sugar and serve for brunch. Serves 4–6.

caramelised vanilla orange

1 cup demerara sugar*
1 cup (8 fl oz) water
1 vanilla bean, split and scraped
4 oranges, peeled and pith removed

Place the sugar, water and vanilla bean in a frying pan over low heat and stir to dissolve the sugar. Increase the heat and allow the syrup to simmer for 10 minutes or until thickened.
Slice the oranges into 2cm (¾ inch) slices. Add the slices to the pan and slowly simmer for 2 minutes each side or until the oranges are coated in the caramelised vanilla syrup. To serve, place the orange slices in bowls and top with a little of the syrup. Serve warm with a glass of dessert wine. Serves 4.

green apple and vanilla snow

6 green apples or 4 cups (32 fl oz) fresh apple juice
¼ cup (2 fl oz) lemon or lime juice
1½ cups (12 fl oz) water
1 vanilla bean, split and scraped
1 cup sugar

Juice the apples (with their skins on) in an electric juicer. Place the apple juice, lemon or lime juice, water and vanilla bean in a saucepan over medium heat and simmer for 4 minutes. Allow to stand for 5 minutes and then remove the vanilla bean. Return the saucepan to low heat, add the sugar and stir until the sugar has dissolved.
Pour the liquid into a flat metal container and freeze for 2 hours. Whisk with a fork and return to the freezer, stirring to break up ice crystals at further 1-hour intervals until the apple and vanilla snow is light and scoopable. Serve in small chilled bowls. Serves 6.

brown sugar vanilla syrup cake

180g (6 oz) butter
1½ cups brown sugar
3 eggs
3 egg yolks
2¼ cups self-raising (self-rising) flour
¾ cup (6 fl oz) milk
vanilla syrup
1 cup sugar
1 cup (8 fl oz) water
1 vanilla bean, split and scraped

Preheat the oven to 180°C (350°F). Place the butter and brown sugar in the bowl of an electric mixer and beat until light and creamy. Add the eggs and yolks one at a time and beat well. Sift the flour over the butter mixture and fold through with the milk.
Pour the mixture into a greased and base-lined 20cm (8 inch) square cake tin and bake for 45 minutes or until cooked when tested with a skewer.
While the cake is cooking, place the sugar, water and vanilla bean in a saucepan and stir over low heat until the sugar has dissolved. Increase the heat and allow the syrup to simmer for 6 minutes.
Leave the cake in its tin for 4 minutes before unmoulding and placing on a serving plate. Pour three-quarters of the hot syrup over the hot cake. Serve with the remaining syrup and thick cream. Serves 10–12.

brown sugar vanilla syrup cake

lemon+lime

2

basics

Two of the most widely enjoyed citrus flavours are lemon and lime. Most cuisines around the word use these fruits to add a sour, acidic flavour to both sweet and savoury recipes.

Lemon, a citrus fruit originating in India (not in the Mediterranean, as is often assumed), was brought to Europe in the 1st century AD by the Romans. From there the Arabs took it to Spain and North Africa, as well as eastwards to China. Christopher Columbus carried the lemon to the Americas on his second voyage in 1493, beginning the New World's love affair with this most popular of fruits.

Limes are the most significant citrus fruit of the tropics. Having their origins somewhere in the region of Malaysia, their cultivation spread to India, the Middle East, China and the West Indies. Cultivation of limes was attempted in southern Europe in medieval times, but the fruit needed a hotter climate than was available there, so its use remained limited. In the West Indies and Central America, however, the introduced lime flourished.

lemon

Lemon is perhaps the most versatile fruit in the citrus family. As a souring agent and a flavour enhancer, it can be used fresh, cooked or preserved, and both the flesh and the skin are edible. There are several varieties of lemon: some are more acidic than others, some have thin skins, others thick skins, and so on. When purchasing lemons, buy those that are dry and heavy for their size. Store lemons in a bowl on the kitchen counter for up to 1 week, or refrigerate for up to 3 weeks.

lime

There are a number of different types of lime, all of them highly acidic. The West Indian or key lime is a small variety that has a true, strong lime flavour. These limes need a very hot climate in order to grow successfully. The more commonly available lime is the Tahitian lime, which is bigger than the key lime and has a less true flavour. These limes are grown in a wide variety of conditions and have a long growing season. Limes can be stored in the refrigerator for up to a week. They show their age by shrivelling their skins and changing their glossy green colour to a pale yellow hue.

rind

The coloured, perfumed and highly flavoured rind of lemon and lime is often used in cooking. When the rind is required, be sure to only remove the coloured rind from the fruit and not the underlying bitter white pith. Rind can be grated on the fine side of a grater, or long shreds can be removed from the fruit with a zester.

kaffir lime leaves

The butterfly-shaped leaves of the kaffir lime tree are used predominantly in Thai cooking. The leaves have a distinct, sweet fragrance and a lightly acidic lime taste. They can be used whole when simmered in curries and soups, or finely shredded for stir-fries or salad dressings. The leaves can be purchased fresh or dry from Asian supermarkets. Excess fresh leaves can be frozen for later use, although the flavour will not be as good. Dry leaves are a poor substitute for the fresh. The trees are available to plant and make attractive shrubs. Pluck the fresh leaves from the tree when needed.

juice

The juice of lemons and limes is easily squeezed from the fruit. If the fruit are old they may have lost some of their moisture, making them hard to juice. Press and roll the fruit on a work surface before squeezing to encourage the inner membranes to release the juice.

juice

lime

lemon

rind

kaffir lime leaves

good ideas

refreshing aid

Make fresh lemonade or limeade by squeezing the fresh juice of either fruit and adding to well-chilled sparkling or still water with lots of ice. Add sugar to taste and serve this cooling and reviving drink immediately.

grate debate

If you hate the mess that is left on the grater after grating citrus rind (and you find most of the rind stays on the grater anyway), use a zester instead and then finely chop the strips of zest.

grilling limes

Grill halved limes, flesh-side down, on a hot grill or barbecue plate when cooking fish or chicken. Squeeze the limes over the meat. The warm juice will have a caramelised flavour and will be easily squeezed from the fruit.

extra juice

To get the most juice from your lemons and limes with the least muscle power, microwave the fruits for 10–15 seconds. This warms and softens the fruit, making the juice flow much more easily.

instant flavour

Add a few kaffir lime leaves when steaming or boiling rice for a great flavour. Add shredded leaves to almost any sauce for vegetables, like oyster sauce with shredded ginger, or a browned butter sauce.

tied to style

Wrap halved lemons or limes in muslin and tie with a piece of string. Serve to your guests when a squeeze of lemon or lime is required. The muslin holds in the pips and also stops the juice from squirting anywhere but the plate.

frozen in time

When lemons and limes are at the peak of their season and in abundant, cheap supply, squeeze the juice, pour into ice-cube containers and freeze. Once frozen, store in an airtight container in the freezer for use at any time.

lime crab salad

preserved lemons and limes

seared tuna with lime crust

lime crab salad

3 cooked crabs or 400g (13 oz) crab meat
lime wedges, for serving
lime salad
1/2 cup (4 fl oz) lime juice
1 tablespoon fish sauce*
2 tablespoons brown sugar
2 Lebanese cucumbers, thinly sliced
1 cup shredded green pawpaw or mango
1/3 cup shredded fresh mint leaves
1/3 cup fresh coriander (cilantro) leaves

To make the lime salad, place the lime juice, fish sauce,
brown sugar, cucumber, pawpaw or mango, mint and
coriander in a bowl and toss to combine. Allow to stand
for 30 minutes to marinate.
Remove the crab meat from the shells. Place the lime salad
on serving plates and top with the crab meat. Serve with
lime wedges. Serves 4.
note – This lime salad is great with cooked prawns,
mussels, lobster or sashimi fish.

warm chicken and lemon couscous salad

4 chicken breast fillets
1 tablespoon olive oil
cracked black pepper
2 lemons, halved
lemon couscous
1 cup couscous*
1 1/4 cups (10 fl oz) boiling chicken stock or water
2 tablespoons butter
2 tablespoons shredded lemon rind
2 tablespoons salted capers*, rinsed
3 tablespoons shredded fresh sage leaves
1/4 cup slivered almonds

Brush the chicken with olive oil and sprinkle with pepper.
Cook the chicken in a hot, preheated grill pan or on a
barbecue for 3 minutes each side or until cooked through.
Set aside. Place the lemons on the grill or barbecue,
cut-side down, and cook for 1 minute.
To make the lemon couscous, place the couscous in a
bowl and pour over the chicken stock or water. Cover
tightly with a lid or plastic wrap and stand for 5 minutes
or until the liquid has been absorbed.
Heat the butter in a large frying pan over medium heat.
Add the lemon rind, capers, sage and almonds and cook
for 7 minutes or until the almonds are lightly toasted.
Add the couscous to the pan and toss to combine.
To serve, pile the lemon couscous onto serving plates
and top with the sliced grilled chicken and grilled lemons.
Serve with salad leaves. Serves 4.

seared tuna with lime crust

375g (12 oz) tuna fillet
1 tablespoon grated lime rind
1/3 cup (2 3/4 fl oz) lime juice
1/4 cup finely chopped fresh dill
2 tablespoons chopped fresh parsley
2 small red chillies, seeded and chopped
2 tablespoons olive oil
sea salt and cracked black pepper
400g (13 oz) fettuccine
1 tablespoon olive oil, extra
100g (3 1/2 oz) baby rocket (arugula) leaves
extra lime juice and olive oil, to serve

Trim the tuna of any sinew and place in a shallow dish.
Combine the lime rind, lime juice, dill, parsley, chilli,
olive oil, salt and pepper and pour over the tuna to coat.
Refrigerate for 20 minutes, turning once.
Cook the pasta in a large saucepan of boiling water until
al dente. Drain. While the pasta is cooking, heat the extra
oil in a frying pan over high heat. Remove the tuna from
the marinade and reserve the liquid. Cook the tuna for
1 minute each side or until well seared, then slice.
To serve, pile the pasta on serving plates and top with
rocket leaves, sliced tuna and the reserved marinade.
Drizzle with a little olive oil and lime juice before serving.
Serves 4.

preserved lemons and limes

1/2 cup coarse rock salt
5 lemons or 12 limes, quartered
5 bay leaves
1 tablespoon black peppercorns
lemon juice or lime juice to fill
3 tablespoons extra-virgin olive oil

Sterilise* a 1-litre (4 cup) screw- or clip-top airtight jar.
Place 1 tablespoon of salt in the bottom of the jar.
Place the lemons or limes in a bowl with the remaining salt
and pummel the ingredients together. Pack the lemons or
limes into the jar with the rind facing out, adding the bay
leaves and peppercorns as you go. Press the ingredients
down firmly as you pack them into the jar. Add enough
lemon or lime juice to the jar to cover the fruit. Top with
olive oil to seal, then seal with the lid.
Allow the jar to stand in a cool, dark place for 1 month
before using the preserved fruit.
To use the preserved lemons or limes, scrape away the
flesh and pith, rinse and finely chop the rind. Add it to
stuffing mixes for lamb, chicken or pork, or fry in a little
olive oil with onions to stir through couscous. Alternatively,
slice the rind and place in the cavity of a whole fish with
fresh herbs before baking. Makes a 1 litre (32 fl oz) jar.

warm chicken and lemon couscous salad

roast lamb with preserved lemon

1 leg of lamb, approximately 1.5kg (3 lb), tunnel boned
1 tablespoon chopped preserved lemon, rind only
  (see page 36)
1/4 cup fresh oregano leaves
2 cloves garlic, sliced
1/2 teaspoon cracked black pepper
1 tablespoon olive oil

Preheat the oven to 200°C (400°F). Trim the lamb of any excess fat. Combine the preserved lemon, oregano, garlic, pepper and oil in a bowl. Stuff the cavity of the lamb with the preserved lemon filling.
Tie the lamb with string to retain its shape and place on a rack in a baking dish. Bake for 45 minutes (medium rare) or until the lamb is cooked to your liking.
Serve the lamb in slices with creamy mashed potatoes and fresh peas. Serves 4–6.

pork dumplings in lime-leaf broth

300g (10 oz) minced pork
1/4 cup (2 fl oz) hoisin sauce*
3 tablespoons chopped coriander (cilantro) leaves
20 dumpling or wonton wrappers*
lime-leaf broth
4 cups (32 fl oz) chicken stock
3 slices ginger
5 kaffir lime leaves, lightly crushed
2 tablespoons soy sauce

To make the pork dumplings, combine the pork, hoisin sauce and coriander leaves. Place 1 tablespoon of the mixture in the centre of each wonton wrapper. Brush a little water around the edges of the wrappers and press the edges together to seal.
To make the lime-leaf broth, place the chicken stock, ginger, lime leaves and soy sauce in a saucepan and simmer over medium–high heat for 3 minutes. Add the dumplings a few at a time and cook for 2–3 minutes or until cooked through. Place the dumplings in bowls and pour some of the broth over to serve. Serve topped with finely shredded lime leaves. Serves 4.
note – You can make the dumplings ahead of time and refrigerate them covered with a slightly damp cloth.

fresh salmon and lime cakes

500g (1 lb) salmon fillet, skin removed
1 egg white
3 tablespoons fine rice flour
2 kaffir lime leaves, shredded
1 tablespoon finely chopped ginger
1 teaspoon wasabi paste*
3 tablespoons chopped fresh chervil* or flat-leaf parsley
oil, to shallow-fry
lime dipping sauce
1/4 cup (2 fl oz) lime juice
1/4 cup (2 fl oz) soy sauce
2 tablespoons brown sugar

To make the salmon cakes, remove any bones from the salmon and chop into 5mm (1/4 inch) dice. Combine the chopped salmon with the egg white, rice flour, lime leaves, ginger, wasabi paste and chopped chervil or parsley.
Heat 1cm (1/2 inch) of oil in a frying pan over medium heat to shallow-fry the cakes. Place 2 tablespoons of the mixture into the hot oil and cook for 35–45 seconds each side, or until lightly golden. Drain on absorbent paper and keep warm in a low oven while you cook the rest.
To make the lime dipping sauce, combine the lime juice, soy sauce and sugar. Serve the dipping sauce with the warm salmon cakes and salad greens as a starter or main meal. Makes 20 small cakes.

pasta with basil and lemon

450g (14 oz) fresh or 350g (11 oz) dry spaghetti or fettuccine
1/3 cup (2 3/4 fl oz) lemon juice
3 tablespoons fruity olive oil
1/2 cup finely grated parmesan cheese
1 cup small fresh basil leaves
1/2 cup small olives
cracked black pepper and sea salt

Cook the pasta in a large saucepan of rapidly boiling water until al dente.
To make the sauce, place the lemon juice and olive oil in a bowl and whisk to combine. Stir through the parmesan, basil, olives, pepper and salt.
Drain the pasta and return to the warm saucepan, then toss with the sauce. Serve immediately. Serves 4.
note – This pasta makes a great meal on its own, or can be served as an accompaniment.

roast lamb with preserved lemon

fresh salmon and lime cakes

pork dumplings in lime-leaf broth

pasta with basil and lemon

veal with lemon

seared river trout with kaffir lime sauce

lemon seared squid

veal with lemon

1 tablespoon olive oil
2 tablespoons butter
1 tablespoon shredded lemon rind
2 tablespoons lemon juice
2 tablespoons fresh oregano leaves
4 thick veal loin steaks
cracked black pepper
lemon wedges, to serve

Place the oil and butter in a frying pan over medium–low heat. Add the lemon rind, lemon juice and oregano leaves and cook for 3 minutes or until the leaves are slightly crisp. Remove the lemon and oregano mix from the frying pan and set aside. Increase the heat to high. Sprinkle the steaks with pepper and add them to the pan. Cook for 2½–3 minutes each side, or until cooked to your liking. Place the veal on a serving plate, sprinkle with the lemon and oregano mix and serve with a pile of steamed greens and the pan juices. Serve with lemon wedges. Serves 4.

seared river trout with kaffir lime sauce

4 river trout fillets
1 tablespoon olive oil
2 tablespoons lime juice
cracked black pepper
mashed potato, to serve
kaffir lime sauce
1 cup (8 fl oz) fish or vegetable stock
4 kaffir lime leaves, shredded
1 cup (8 fl oz) cream
1 tablespoon lime juice

To make the kaffir lime sauce, place the stock, lime leaves, cream and lime juice in a saucepan over medium–low heat. Allow the sauce to simmer until reduced by half.
Wash the trout and pat dry. Heat a large frying pan over medium–high heat. Add the oil, lime and pepper and cook for 30 seconds. Add the trout, skin-side down, and cook for 2 minutes each side or until cooked to your liking.
To serve, place a pile of creamy mashed potato on serving plates and top with the trout. Spoon over the kaffir lime sauce and serve. Serves 4.

lemon seared squid

12 small squid
1/3 cup (2¾ fl oz) lemon juice
1 tablespoon olive oil
2 cloves garlic, finely chopped
1 tablespoon fresh lemon thyme, finely chopped
1 teaspoon sea salt
cracked black pepper

Clean the squid and cut the bodies in half. Cut a few slashes in the squid with the tip of a sharp knife. Combine the lemon juice, olive oil, garlic, thyme, salt and pepper and pour over the squid. Refrigerate to marinate for at least 30 minutes but preferably 1½ hours. Preheat a grill pan, barbecue plate or frying pan over high heat. Cook the squid for 20–30 seconds each side. Serve with salad greens or thin-fried potatoes. Serves 4.

spaghetti with lime and rocket

[handwritten: VERY GOOD 12.26.05]

450g (14 oz) spaghetti *[handwritten: 3 oz]*
2 tablespoons fruity extra-virgin olive oil *[handwritten: more ½ T — maybe Paul Newman dressing]*
1 tablespoon shredded lime rind *[handwritten: 1 tea,]*
2 cloves garlic, crushed *[handwritten: ½ clove]*
1 red chilli, seeded and chopped *[handwritten: sprinkled]*
2 tablespoons salted capers*, rinsed *[handwritten: ½ T]*
8 slices prosciutto*, chopped *[handwritten: more 2 slices]*
150g (5 oz) rocket (arugula), shredded *[handwritten: 1 oz+]*
3 tablespoons lime juice *[handwritten: 1 T]*
150g (5 oz) soft marinated feta* in oil *[handwritten: 1 oz — try to find]*
[handwritten: little 2 or 3 canned plum tomatoes on the side]

Cook the spaghetti in a large saucepan of rapidly boiling water until al dente. Drain.
While the spaghetti is cooking, heat the oil in a large saucepan over medium heat. Add the lime rind, garlic, chilli and capers and cook for 1 minute or until fragrant. Add the prosciutto and cook, stirring for 2 minutes or until the prosciutto is crisp. Add the spaghetti to the pan and toss to coat and heat through.
To serve, toss the rocket and lime juice through the pasta and pile into serving bowls. Top with the marinated feta, *[handwritten: — try chevre]* a little of its oil and cracked black pepper. Serves 4.
note – If prosciutto is not available, substitute with bacon rashers. Remove the rinds before chopping.

spaghetti with lime and rocket

lime and lemongrass beef

600g (1¼ lb) beef fillet
1 tablespoon oil
1 stalk lemongrass*, white part only, shredded
4 kaffir lime leaves, shredded
1 tablespoon shredded ginger
⅓ cup (2¾ fl oz) soy sauce
¼ cup (2 fl oz) lime juice
2 tablespoons brown sugar
steamed greens, such as bok choy*, beans or asparagus

Preheat the oven to 180°C (350°F). Trim the beef fillet
of any sinew or fat and tie with string to hold its shape.
Heat the oil in a frying pan over high heat and cook the
beef for 2 minutes each side or until well sealed. Place
the beef on a baking tray and bake for 12–15 minutes.
While the beef is cooking, place the lemongrass, lime
leaves and ginger in the frying pan the beef was seared in.
Cook for 1 minute over medium–high heat. Add the soy
sauce, lime juice and brown sugar and stir for 1 minute.
To serve, slice the beef and place on the steamed greens.
Top with the sauce and serve. Serves 4.

kingfish lime and coconut ceviche

500g (1 lb) kingfish fillet (or other firm white fish),
  skin removed
½ cup (4 fl oz) lime or lemon juice
½ cup (4 fl oz) coconut cream
2 mild red chillies, seeded and chopped
¼ cup (2 fl oz) lime or lemon juice, extra
⅓ cup fresh coriander (cilantro) leaves
2 tablespoons shredded fresh basil leaves
sea salt and cracked black pepper
salad greens, to serve

Remove the bones from the kingfish and cut into thin,
sashimi-style slices. Place the fish in a glass or ceramic
bowl with the lime or lemon juice and refrigerate for 2 hours
or until the fish turns opaque and appears cooked. Drain.
Combine the fish with the coconut cream, chilli, extra lime
or lemon juice, coriander, basil, salt and pepper. Chill for
up to 4 hours before serving. Serve the marinated fish with
salad greens as a starter or summer lunch. Serves 4.

lime fried fish

1 tablespoon olive oil
1 tablespoon butter
3 limes, peeled and sliced
2 tablespoons whole fresh sage leaves
4 x 185g (6 oz) pieces firm white fish such as blue eye cod
sea salt and cracked black pepper

Heat the oil and butter in a large frying pan over medium–
high heat. Add the lime slices and cook for 1 minute each
side. Add the sage leaves and cook for a further minute.
Remove the sage leaves and lime slices from the pan,
then add the fish and cook for 3 minutes each side or until
tender. Sprinkle salt and pepper over the fish and serve
with the sage leaves, lime slices and crisp potatoes.
Serves 4.

lemon roasted chicken

1.6kg (3¼ lb) chicken
2 lemons, chopped
4 cloves garlic
3 sprigs fresh rosemary
1 tablespoon olive oil
1 tablespoon lemon juice
cracked black pepper

Preheat the oven to 200°C (400°F). Wash the chicken
and pat dry. Fill the cavity of the chicken with the lemon,
garlic and rosemary. Place the chicken on a metal rack in
a baking dish and rub with the olive oil, lemon juice and
pepper. Roast for 45–60 minutes or until the chicken is
cooked through.
To serve, cut the chicken into pieces and serve with a
peppery rocket salad and garlic mayonnaise (see recipe
page 88). Serves 4.
note – This recipe is equally good made with limes.

lime and lemongrass beef

lime fried fish

kingfish lime and coconut ceviche

lemon roasted chicken

lemon yoghurt with blueberries

lime tart

lemon yoghurt with blueberries

2 cups (16 fl oz) thick plain yoghurt
1/4 cup icing (confectioners') sugar, sifted
1 tablespoon very finely grated lemon rind
3/4 cup (6 fl oz) cream
2 teaspoons gelatine
200g (6 1/2 oz) blueberries

Place the yoghurt, sugar and lemon rind in a bowl and mix to combine. Allow to stand until the mixture reaches room temperature. Place the cream in a saucepan over low heat and heat until hot. Sprinkle with the gelatine and stir for 2 minutes until the gelatine is dissolved. Add the cream and gelatine mix to the yoghurt and stir to combine. Place half the blueberries into four 3/4-cup (6 fl oz) capacity ramekins or moulds, pour in the cream and yoghurt mix and refrigerate for 3 hours or until firm. Serve with the remaining blueberries. These are great for brunch or dessert. Serves 4.

lime tart

1 quantity sweet shortcrust pastry*, or 375g (12 oz) ready-prepared pastry
lime filling
1 cup caster (superfine) sugar
4 eggs
1 cup (8 fl oz) cream
1 cup (8 fl oz) lime juice

Preheat the oven to 180°C (350°F). Roll out the pastry to fit a 25cm (10 inch) removable-base tart tin. Prick a few holes in the pastry and line with non-stick baking paper. Fill with rice or baking weights and bake for 10 minutes. Remove the baking weights and paper and bake for a further 10 minutes. This process is called blind baking and will keep the tart shell crisp when filled with a wet filling. To make the lime filling, place the sugar, eggs, cream and lime juice in a bowl and mix to combine. Skim the top of the mixture to remove any bubbles or foam. Pour into the tart shell, reduce the oven to 160°C (315°F) and bake for 20–25 minutes or until the filling is just set. Refrigerate the tart until firm.
To serve, cut into wedges and serve with thick cream or ice cream. Serves 8.
note – You can swap the lime juice for lemon juice or blood orange juice.

lemon curd cake   simple lime puddings

sweet lemon brown-buttered apples

lemon curd cake

125g (4 oz) butter
1 cup caster (superfine) sugar
4 eggs
1 cup almond meal (ground almonds)
2 cups self-raising (self-rising) flour
thick cream, to serve
lemon curd
90g (3 oz) butter
1/2 cup (4 fl oz) lemon juice
1 cup caster (superfine) sugar
2 eggs

Preheat the oven to 160°C (315°F). Place the butter and sugar in the bowl of an electric mixer and beat until light and creamy. Gradually add the eggs and beat well. Lightly stir through the almond meal and flour with a wooden spoon.
Spoon the mixture into a lined 8 x 26cm (3½ x 10½ inch) loaf tin and bake for 30–45 minutes or until golden and cooked when tested with a skewer. Cool the cake on a wire rack and then slice into three layers.
To make the lemon curd, place the butter, lemon juice, sugar and eggs in an ovenproof bowl over a saucepan of simmering water. Stir for 6–9 minutes or until the mixture thickens. Remove the bowl from the heat and cool.
To assemble, spread each layer of the cake with lemon curd. Refrigerate until ready to serve. Serve in slices with thick cream. Serves 12–14.

simple lime puddings

2 teaspoons grated lime rind
1/2 cup (4 fl oz) lime juice
1½ cups caster (superfine) sugar
60g (2 oz) butter
1 cup (8 fl oz) milk
1/2 cup (4 fl oz) cream
3 eggs, separated
1/4 cup self-raising (self-rising) flour

Preheat the oven to 180°C (350°F). Place the lime rind, lime juice, sugar, butter, milk, cream, egg yolks and flour in the bowl of an electric mixer and beat until smooth. Place the egg whites in another clean bowl of an electric mixer and beat until soft peaks form. Fold the egg whites into the lime mixture. Spoon the mixture into six 1-cup (8 fl oz) capacity ovenproof dishes. Place the dishes in a baking tray and fill with enough water to come halfway up the sides of the dishes. Bake for 30 minutes or until the tops are puffed and golden. Serve warm. Serves 6.

sweet lemon brown-buttered apples

4 sweet red apples, halved
60g (2 oz) butter, chopped
1/3 cup demerara sugar*
lemon brown butter
125g (4 oz) butter
1/4 cup (2 fl oz) lemon juice
4 tablespoons sugar

Preheat the oven to 180°C (350°F). Place the apples in a baking dish, cut-side up, and top with butter and demerara sugar. Bake for 30 minutes, basting frequently until the apples are soft.
To make the lemon brown butter, place the butter in a saucepan over medium–low heat. Allow the butter to slowly simmer until it smells nutty and has turned golden brown. Remove from the heat and add the lemon juice and sugar. Return to the heat and stir for 2 minutes.
To serve, place the apples on serving plates and spoon over the lemon brown butter. Serve warm with caramel ice cream or thick cream. Serves 4.

classic baked lemon cheesecake

base
85g (3 oz) plain sweet shortbread biscuits
1/2 cup almond meal (ground almonds)
45g (1½ oz) butter, melted
topping
600g (1¼ lb) cream cheese
1 cup sugar
3/4 cup (6 fl oz) sour cream
6 eggs
1 tablespoon finely grated lemon rind

Preheat the oven to 140°C (275°F). To make the base, place the biscuits in a food processor and process until smooth. Place in a mixing bowl with the almond meal and butter and mix to combine. Press the mixture over the base of a 22cm (9 inch) round springform pan and refrigerate until required.
To make the topping, place the cream cheese, sugar and sour cream in a food processor and process until smooth. Then add the eggs and lemon rind and process until well combined.
Pour the topping over the base in the pan and bake in the preheated oven for 1 hour or until the topping is just firm to touch. Cool in the tin and serve in slices with lemon curd (see lemon curd cake) or with sliced fruit. Serves 12.

classic baked lemon cheesecake

3

ginger

basics

Ginger is thought to have originated in South-East Asia. Its hot, spicy and clean flavours have, however, carried it much further afield over the course of the centuries. In ancient times it was a highly prized Eastern import to the Roman Empire, where it was used predominantly for medicinal purposes. In medieval England, ginger was almost as common as pepper (in fact, the word 'spice' was synonymous with ginger), but it was also eaten in a preserved or glacé form as a sweet. Cooks of the Middle East, Africa and South America have long used ginger, especially in its ground form, but it is in Asian cuisine that this tuberous rhizome has flourished.

Eaten sliced, juiced, grated, ground, minced or mashed, or preserved in vinegar or sugar, ginger is an essential ingredient in a countless array of dishes from all over the world.

galangal

A member of the same family as the ginger rhizome, galangal is sometimes called greater galangal or Thai ginger. It has trimmed dry stems attached to a pinkish, knobbly root. Galangal is tougher than ginger and needs to be peeled before shredding or grating. Its flavour is more lemony and peppery than that of pure ginger. Use only the freshest product, as older galangal gets very tough and hard to cut and grate.

ginger

Young ginger has pink tips and a paper-thin skin that is easily rubbed off before chopping or shredding. When cooking, tender crisp ginger is preferred to the older, tougher and more pungent root, as the young ginger is less fibrous, making it easier to shred or grate. It also has a more subdued flavour. If using older ginger, peel or cut away the thick skin with a knife or vegetable peeler, and remember to use less, since the flavour will be hotter.

glacé ginger

Small pieces of peeled ginger that have been slightly dried and soaked in a heavy sugar syrup are described as glacé (from the French, meaning 'iced'). Glacé ginger is either sold in the syrup or with a crystallised sugar coating. Sweets and cakes that require ginger will benefit from the addition of finely chopped or minced glacé ginger rather than powdered ginger, as the taste is truer.

powdered ginger

This is dry ginger that has been ground to form a fine powder. It is often used when baking sweets or biscuits. For a more superior ginger taste, you might find it preferable to use finely chopped glacé ginger. If using powdered ginger, however, purchase in small quantities, as the flavour diminishes or stales over time.

pickled ginger

This Japanese speciality consists of very thinly sliced or shredded ginger that has been pickled in a sweetened vinegar. It is usually pink, the colour occurring as a result of a natural reaction between the ginger and the vinegar. Pickled ginger is an indispensable accompaniment to sashimi, or thin fillets of raw fish. There are many different types and names for pickled ginger, but all are known colloquially as 'gari'.

powdered ginger

galangal

ginger

glacé ginger

pickled ginger

55

good ideas

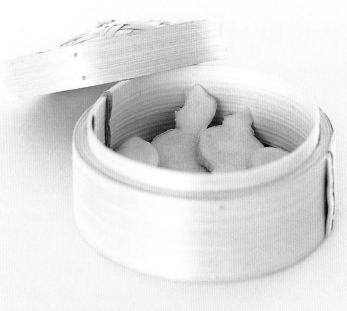

ginger steam

Line the base of a bamboo steamer with sliced ginger before steaming fish or chicken to give a subtle ginger flavour to the food.

marinade

Ginger makes a great marinade. Combine ginger with sesame and vegetable oil, chopped chillies, cracked black pepper and chopped fresh herbs.

flavoured oil

Gently heat slices of galangal or ginger in plenty of olive oil. Cool and pour into bottles. Store in the refrigerator and use as a flavour base for stir-fries, dressings and marinades.

health tea

Infuse slices of ginger and lemon rind in boiling water for 3 minutes and add a little honey to sweeten. This tea is also great to sip if you have a cold.

pickled ginger salad

For a fresh zing to a salad, mix sliced pickled ginger through chilled noodles. Toss with a citrus-based dressing.

cleanse

A combination of apple, carrot, pineapple or melon juice and a small cube of ginger is said to cleanse the body. Serve the juice over crushed ice.

fried ginger

Deep-fry finely shredded ginger in hot oil until golden and crisp, then drain. Use as a zingy garnish to salads, noodles or Asian soups.

ginger

fried ginger and peanut salad

galangal soup with chicken

ginger noodle salad with seared tuna

fried ginger and peanut salad

1/2 cup chopped unsalted peanuts
2 small red chillies, seeded and chopped
1/4 cup brown sugar
2 tablespoons water
oil, for deep-frying
1 cup shredded ginger
200g (61/2 oz) dry rice-stick noodles*
1/2 cup fresh coriander (cilantro) leaves
1/2 cup fresh mint leaves
350g (11 oz) cooked Chinese barbecued pork*, sliced
2 tablespoons soy sauce
2 tablespoons lime juice

Place the peanuts, chillies, sugar and water in a frying pan over high heat and cook, stirring frequently, until the peanuts are sticky and coated. Set aside.
Heat the oil in a saucepan over medium–high heat. Add the shredded ginger and cook for 3 minutes or until golden and crisp. Drain on absorbent paper.
Place the noodles in a saucepan of boiling water and cook for 2 minutes or until soft. Drain and cool.
Toss the noodles with the peanut mixture, coriander and mint and place on serving plates. Top with the barbecued pork and sprinkle with soy sauce and lime juice. Finally, top with the fried ginger. Serves 4.

galangal soup with chicken

4 cups (32 fl oz) chicken stock
11/2 cups (12 fl oz) water
1/2 cup (4 fl oz) Chinese cooking wine* or sherry
10 slices galangal
1 stalk lemongrass*, bruised
1 small red chilli, seeded and chopped
3 chicken breast fillets, thinly sliced
150g (5 oz) fresh rice or egg noodles*
4 small wedges Chinese cabbage

Place the chicken stock, water, Chinese cooking wine, galangal, lemongrass and chilli in a saucepan over medium heat. Cover and simmer for 5 minutes or until the soup is well flavoured.
Add the chicken and simmer for 3 minutes. Add the noodles and cabbage and cook for a further 2 minutes. Remove the lemongrass and galangal from the soup.
To serve, ladle the soup into 4 deep bowls. Best eaten with spoons and chopsticks. Serves 4.

ginger noodle salad with seared tuna

200g (61/2 oz) dry somen noodles*
1 teaspoon sesame oil*
1 tablespoon vegetable oil
2 tablespoons lime juice
1 teaspoon wasabi paste*
1/4 cup pickled ginger, drained
1/4 cup snipped garlic chives
375g (12 oz) sashimi* tuna
black sesame seeds*, to coat
soy sauce and wasabi paste*, to serve

Place the noodles in a saucepan of boiling water and cook for 2 minutes or until soft. Drain and cool under running water, then drain again. Combine the sesame oil, vegetable oil, lime juice and wasabi paste and pour this mixture over the noodles. Add the pickled ginger and garlic chives and toss to combine.
Press the tuna into the sesame seeds. Cook in a nonstick frying pan over high heat for 1 minute each side or until just seared. Cut into thick slices.
To serve, divide the noodles among bowls and top with the tuna. Serve with soy sauce and wasabi in dipping bowls. Serves 4.

chicken poached in ginger broth

4 chicken breast fillets
300g (10 oz) snake beans, halved
ginger broth
2 tablespoons shredded ginger
4 spring (green) onions, chopped
1 star anise
2 tablespoons soy sauce
4 cups (32 fl oz) chicken stock

To make the ginger broth, place the shredded ginger, spring onions, star anise, soy sauce and chicken stock in a deep frying pan or wok over medium–high heat and allow to simmer for 3 minutes.
Add the chicken breasts to the frying pan and simmer slowly for 6 minutes each side. Remove the chicken from the pan and set aside. Place the snake beans into the broth and cook for 4 minutes or until just tender.
To serve, place the broth and snake beans into shallow bowls. Slice each chicken breast into 3 pieces and place on top of the snake beans. Serve immediately. Serves 4.

chicken poached in ginger broth

ginger-grilled beef with sweet potato salad

8 thin beef steaks, 80g (2¾ oz) each

2 tablespoons finely grated ginger

2 tablespoons olive oil

cracked black pepper

200g (6½ oz) baby English spinach leaves

sweet potato salad

750g (1½ lb) orange sweet potatoes (kumera), peeled

2 tablespoons olive oil

sea salt and cracked black pepper

⅓ cup sweet chilli sauce

2 teaspoons grated ginger, extra

2 tablespoons lemon juice

1 tablespoon olive oil, extra

Trim the steaks and place in a shallow dish. Combine the ginger, oil and pepper and pour over the steaks. Allow to marinate for 30 minutes, turning once.

Preheat the oven to 180°C (350°F). To make the sweet potato salad, cut the sweet potatoes into large pieces and place in a baking dish. Add the oil, salt and pepper to the dish and toss to coat. Bake for 30 minutes or until the sweet potatoes are golden and soft.

Cook the marinated steaks on a hot, preheated grill or barbecue for 1–2 minutes each side or until cooked to your liking.

To serve, place the spinach leaves on serving plates and top with the roasted sweet potato and steak slices. Combine the sweet chilli sauce, extra ginger, lemon juice and extra oil and pour over the salad. Serves 4.

pork, ginger and lime stir-fry

1 tablespoon peanut oil

2 tablespoons shredded ginger

1 teaspoon cracked black pepper

6 kaffir lime leaves, shredded

2 cloves garlic, sliced

600g (1¼ lb) pork fillet, trimmed and sliced

3 tablespoons lime juice

2 tablespoons brown sugar

3 tablespoons sweet chilli sauce

6 bok choy*, quartered and steamed

Heat the oil in a frying pan or wok over medium–high heat. Add the ginger, pepper, lime leaves and garlic and cook for 1 minute. Add the pork and stir-fry for 5 minutes or until well browned. Add the lime juice, brown sugar and sweet chilli sauce to the pan and stir-fry for a further 3 minutes or until the sauce has thickened slightly. Toss through the bok choy and cook for 1 minute.

To serve, place steamed rice in bowls and top with the pork stir-fry. Serves 4.

soy and galangal fish

2 teaspoons sesame oil*

1 tablespoon peanut oil

2 tablespoons shredded galangal

2 large mild red chillies, shredded

½ cup (4 fl oz) salt-reduced soy sauce

⅓ cup (2¾ fl oz) Chinese cooking wine*

2 tablespoons brown sugar

4 x 180g (6 oz) white fish fillets

steamed rice, to serve

Heat the oils in a large frying pan over medium–high heat. Add the galangal and chillies and cook for 2 minutes or until crisp. Add the soy sauce, cooking wine and sugar to the pan and simmer for 1 minute or until the sauce has thickened slightly.

Add the fish fillets to the pan and cook in the sauce for 3 minutes each side or until cooked.

To serve, place piles of steamed rice on serving plates and top with the fish and the pan sauce. Serve with steamed greens or asparagus. Serves 4.

prawn and ginger dumplings

300g (10 oz) green (raw) prawn meat, finely chopped

1 tablespoon grated ginger

1 tablespoon lemon juice

1 teaspoon sesame oil*

20 dumpling or wonton wrappers

2 cups (16 fl oz) fish stock

dipping sauce

¼ cup (2 fl oz) lemon juice

2 tablespoons chilli sauce

1 tablespoon sugar

Place the prawn meat, ginger, lemon juice and sesame oil in a bowl and mix to combine. Place a tablespoon of the mixture onto a dumpling or wonton wrapper and brush the edge with water. Press the edges firmly to seal.

To cook the dumplings, place the stock in a saucepan over medium heat and allow to rapidly simmer. Place a few dumplings into the stock and cook for 3 minutes or until the dumplings are cooked through. Set aside and keep warm while you cook the remaining dumplings.

To make the dipping sauce, combine the lemon juice, chilli sauce and sugar and serve in a small bowl with the warm dumplings. Serves 4 as a starter.

ginger-grilled beef with sweet potato salad

pork, ginger and lime stir-fry

prawn and ginger dumplings

soy and galangal fish

pumpkin and ginger tart

1 quantity sweet shortcrust pastry*, or 375g (12 oz)
  ready-prepared pastry
filling
2 cups puréed pumpkin (Japanese* or butternut)
¾ cup brown sugar
1½ cups (12 fl oz) cream
2 eggs
2 tablespoons plain (all-purpose) flour
1 teaspoon ground cinnamon
2 teaspoons finely grated ginger
½ teaspoon grated nutmeg

Preheat the oven to 200°C (400°F). Roll out the pastry
on a lightly floured surface until 3mm (⅛ inch) thick.
Line a deep 23cm (9 inch) tart ring or removable-base
deep 23cm (9 inch) tart tin with the pastry and trim.
Prick the base and side of the pastry, line with non-stick
baking paper and fill with baking weights or rice. Bake the
pastry case for 5 minutes, then remove the weights and
paper and cook for a further 5 minutes or until golden.
To make the filling, place the pumpkin, sugar, cream,
eggs, flour, cinnamon, ginger and nutmeg in a food
processor and process until just combined. Pour into
the pastry case. Reduce the oven temperature to 180°C
(350°F) and bake for 25–30 minutes or until the filling is
just set. Serve with thick cream. Serves 8–10.

ginger snaps

60g (2 oz) butter
½ cup (4 fl oz) golden syrup
1 teaspoon bicarbonate of soda
1¼ cups plain (all-purpose) flour
1 tablespoon finely chopped glacé ginger
½ cup brown sugar

Preheat the oven to 160°C (315°F). Place the butter
and golden syrup in a saucepan and stir over low heat
until the butter has melted. Add the bicarbonate of soda
and allow to fizz. Remove from the heat.
Place the flour, ginger and sugar in a bowl and mix to
combine. Add the butter mixture and mix to combine.
Drop tablespoons of the mixture onto baking trays lined
with non-stick baking paper. Bake for 12–15 minutes
or until firm. Cool on wire racks. Makes 16.

pumpkin and ginger tart   ginger snaps

4 chilli

basics

One of the most important spices in Asia, chilli is in fact a native of Mexico. The Spanish conquistadors took this fiery fruit to Europe in the 16th century, along with its close relative the capsicum, and from there it gained a foothold in the Balkans and Middle East. But responsibility for the spread of the chilli to Asia lies in the hands of the Portuguese, who introduced it to India. There it gained immediate popularity, its fame spreading eastwards to South-East Asia.

Chillies can be red or green (and occasionally purple or dark brown), small or large, pointed or round, and, most significantly, hot or mild. The general guide to gauging the heat of a chilli is: the smaller the chilli, the bigger the kick. Don't be fooled by colour, either. The most innocent-looking of cool-green small chillies can carry a hefty punch, whilst the largest and reddest can be relatively mild. Bear in mind also that long chillies are hotter than round ones.

large red chillies

These are the gentle giants of the chilli world, having all the flavour but not as much heat as their smaller sisters. Remove the seeds and the inner membrane for an even more mellow chilli taste.

small red chillies

These are the fire of the chilli world. The most common small red chilli is the bird's-eye chilli, which is most frequently used in Thai and Chinese cooking. To remove some of the heat but not the flavour, remove the seeds and the white membrane attached to the seeds before chopping.

large green chillies

Like their red counterparts, large green chillies have less heat than small green ones. All chillies are hotter near the stem than at the tip, so when testing a green chilli for heat, make sure you taste the whole lot: seeds, membrane and base. Just touch a small piece on your tongue and, if the heat burns, cool your mouth with some yoghurt, cucumber or sugar.

small green chillies

Often mistaken for having less heat than red chillies, green chillies can in fact be very hot. They are simply chillies that are unripe and haven't yet turned red. The small green chillies commonly used in Thai cooking can be very hot.

dried chillies

Available in flakes or powdered, dried chillies are handy to have in the cupboard if you can't find the fresh. Dried chillies vary in heat, so place a tiny bit on the end of your tongue to test before using in any quantity in a recipe.

capsicums

Also known as sweet or bell peppers, these are the most mildly flavoured members of the *Capsicum* family. Green capsicums, which ripen and turn to red capsicums, are the most common, but there are also yellow and purple capsicums. To prepare the capsicums, remove the green stem and seeds before chopping.

dried chillies

capsicum

large red chilli

small green chillies

large green chilli

small red chillies

good ideas

chill out

To remove some of the heat from chillies, soak them in cold water for 30 minutes before scraping away the seeds and membranes and chopping up the flesh.

on the side

For a simple side dish, fill halved capsicums (peppers) with a mixture of crumbled goats' cheese, fresh oregano leaves, fresh breadcrumbs and chopped tomatoes. Place in a 180°C (350°F) oven and bake for 30 minutes or until soft and golden.

chilli paste

Make a chilli paste by placing seeded chillies, fresh coriander (cilantro), cumin seeds and grated ginger in a food processor with a little peanut oil. Spread the paste on meats before cooking them, or use as a flavour base for stir-fries or marinades.

chunky salsa

To make this simple and tasty salsa, combine chopped capsicum (pepper), chilli, tomato and half a red onion with lime juice, black pepper and chopped coriander (cilantro). Serve with grilled meats or as a dip.

strung out

Drying excess chillies for later use is easy. Thread a large needle with string, then thread the needle through the tops of the chillies. Tie them somewhere breezy to dry. Store in an airtight container.

roasted capsicums

Place whole capsicums (peppers) on a tray under a hot grill. Cook, turning occasionally, until the skins are black. Place in a plastic bag and seal. When cool, the skins will be easy to remove. Cut the capsicums open and remove the seeds.

sweet chilli sauce

Remove the seeds from 8 large chillies and chop. Place in a saucepan with 1 cup (8 fl oz) of vinegar, 1 cup of water and 2 cups of sugar and simmer over medium heat for 25 minutes or until the sauce thickens slightly.

beef with marinated pawpaw and green chilli

slow-simmered chilli pork

salmon with crisp chilli salad

beef with marinated pawpaw and green chilli

750g (1½ lb) rump steak, trimmed
oil, for brushing
cracked black pepper
salad greens
marinated pawpaw and green chilli
350g (11 oz) green (unripe) pawpaw
2 green chillies, seeded and chopped
1 cup shredded fresh mint leaves
½ cup fresh coriander (cilantro) leaves
3 tablespoons lemon juice
2 tablespoons fish sauce*
2 tablespoons sugar

To make the marinated pawpaw and green chilli, finely shred the pawpaw and combine it with the chillies, mint, coriander, lemon juice, fish sauce and sugar. Allow to marinate for 15 minutes.
Brush the steak with a little oil and sprinkle with pepper. Cook the steak on a hot grill or barbecue for 2 minutes each side, or until cooked to your liking.
To serve, place salad greens on serving plates. Slice the steak thinly and pile on top, then top with the marinated pawpaw. Serve with lemon wedges. Serves 4.

slow-simmered chilli pork

1 tablespoon olive oil
2 onions, chopped
2 cloves garlic, sliced
2 tablespoons shredded ginger
4 large red chillies, seeded and shredded
750g (1½ lb) diced pork leg
1½ cups (12 fl oz) Chinese cooking wine*
½ cup (4 fl oz) salt-reduced soy sauce
1 cup (8 fl oz) beef stock
2 tablespoons palm sugar* or brown sugar
½ cup fresh coriander (cilantro) leaves

Heat the oil in a large saucepan over medium–high heat. Add the onions, garlic, ginger and chillies and cook for 4 minutes or until soft. Add the pork to the pan and cook, stirring, for 5 minutes or until sealed.
Add the cooking wine, soy sauce, beef stock and sugar to the pan. Reduce the heat and simmer, uncovered, stirring occasionally, for 50 minutes or until the pork is tender.
To serve, stir the coriander leaves through the pork and serve with steamed rice and greens. Serves 4.

salmon with crisp chilli salad

4 x 200g pieces salmon fillet
2 tablespoons lime juice
crisp chilli salad
2–3 tablespoons peanut oil
4 large green chillies, seeded and shredded
4 large red chillies, seeded and shredded
3 tablespoons shredded ginger
½ cup fresh Thai basil
½ cup fresh mint
½ cup fresh coriander (cilantro) leaves
2 kaffir lime leaves, shredded

To make the crisp chilli salad, heat the oil in a large frying pan over high heat. Add the green and red chillies and ginger and cook for 5–7 minutes or until the ingredients are crisp. Remove from the pan with a slotted spoon and drain on absorbent paper. Set aside.
To cook the salmon fillets, use the same frying pan and oil that the chillies and ginger were cooked in. Reduce the heat to medium, add the salmon to the pan and cook for 2 minutes each side or until cooked to your liking.
To serve, toss the chillies and ginger with the basil, mint, coriander and shredded lime leaves. Place the salmon on serving plates, top with the chilli salad and drizzle over the lime juice. Serves 4.

chilli-crusted lamb cutlets with cucumber yoghurt

8–12 lamb cutlets
4 large red chillies, seeded and chopped
2 spring (green) onions, chopped
2 tablespoons lemon juice
½ cup fresh coriander (cilantro) leaves
1 tablespoon olive oil
cucumber yoghurt
1 cup (8 fl oz) thick plain yoghurt
½ Lebanese cucumber, finely chopped
3 tablespoons chopped fresh mint
sea salt and cracked black pepper

To make the cucumber yoghurt, place the yoghurt, cucumber, mint, sea salt and cracked black pepper in a bowl and stir to combine.
Trim the lamb cutlets of any excess fat. Place the chillies, spring onions, lemon juice, coriander and olive oil in a food processor and process until roughly chopped.
Spread the paste over both sides of the cutlets. Place the cutlets on a baking tray and cook under a hot grill for 3–4 minutes each side or until cooked to your liking.
Place the lamb cutlets on plates and serve with the cucumber yoghurt, flatbread and salad leaves. Serves 4.

chilli-crusted lamb cutlets with cucumber yoghurt

simmered chicken dumplings in chilli broth

3 chicken breast fillets, chopped
1 egg white
1 small red chilli, seeded and chopped
2 tablespoons chopped fresh Thai basil
1 tablespoon grated ginger
chilli broth
6 cups (48 fl oz) chicken stock
4 kaffir lime leaves, shredded
1 large red chilli, sliced
¼ cup (2 fl oz) Chinese cooking wine* or sherry
2 tablespoons soy sauce

To make the dumplings, place the chicken fillets, egg white, chilli, basil and ginger in a food processor and process until the mixture is minced together. Roll 2 tablespoons of the mixture into a ball, place on a tray and repeat with the remaining mixture.
To make the chilli broth, place the chicken stock, lime leaves, chilli, cooking wine and soy sauce in a saucepan over medium–high heat. Allow to simmer. Place half the dumplings into the broth and stir gently to separate them. Cook, covered, for 5 minutes or until the dumplings are tender. Remove the dumplings and keep warm while you cook the remaining dumplings in the same way.
To serve, place the dumplings in bowls and pour over the broth. Serves 4.

chilli baked beans

250g (8 oz) dried black-eye beans
1 tablespoon olive oil
3 red chillies, seeded and chopped
2 onions, chopped
16 slices pancetta*, chopped
1 tablespoon fresh sage leaves
2 cloves garlic, sliced
2 x 440g (14 oz) cans peeled tomatoes
2 cups (16 fl oz) vegetable or beef stock
¼ cup chopped fresh flat-leaf parsley
2 tablespoons lemon juice
sea salt and cracked black pepper

Place the beans in a large bowl of water and allow to soak for 3–4 hours or overnight.
Preheat the oven to 180°C (350°F). Heat the oil in a frying pan over medium heat. Add the chillies, onions, pancetta, sage and garlic and cook for 3 minutes or until soft.
Place the onion mixture, together with the tomatoes, stock and the drained beans, in an ovenproof dish. Place in the oven and bake, covered, for 1 hour or until the beans are soft. Stir through the parsley, lemon juice, salt and pepper and serve with crusty bread. Serves 4.

roast capsicum soup

4 red capsicums (peppers), halved and seeded
8 tomatoes, halved
olive oil, for brushing
3 cups (24 fl oz) vegetable stock
2 tablespoons shredded fresh basil
sea salt and cracked black pepper
shaved parmesan cheese, to serve

Preheat the oven to 200°C (400°F). Place the capsicums on a baking tray, skin-side up, and on a separate tray place the tomatoes, flesh-side up. Brush the capsicums and tomatoes with a little oil and bake for 40 minutes or until the capsicum skins are black and the tomatoes are soft. Place the capsicums in a plastic bag, tie the top and leave for 5 minutes, then peel away the skins. Place the capsicum flesh and tomatoes in a food processor or blender and process with a little of the vegetable stock until smooth. Place the mixture in a saucepan with the remaining stock and heat over medium heat until hot. Stir through the basil and serve in deep bowls sprinkled with salt, pepper and parmesan cheese. Serve with warm bread. Serves 6 as a starter or 4 as a main.

sticky chilli chicken

1.5kg (3 lb) chicken pieces
chilli sauce
3 red chillies, seeded and chopped
1 tablespoon grated ginger
2 cups (16 fl oz) water
⅔ cup (2¾ fl oz) soy sauce
½ cup (4 fl oz) white wine vinegar
⅔ cup sugar
½ cup chopped fresh coriander (cilantro) leaves

To make the chilli sauce, place the chillies, ginger, water, soy sauce, vinegar and sugar in a deep frying pan over medium heat and allow to simmer for 3 minutes. Add the chicken pieces and cook, covered, for 35 minutes, turning occasionally. Remove the lid from the pan and continue cooking for 25 minutes, turning the chicken until it is cooked and well coated in the chilli sauce.
Stir through the coriander leaves and serve with steamed rice and greens. Serves 4.

simmered chicken dumplings in chilli broth

roast capsicum soup

chilli baked beans

sticky chilli chicken

chilli

pasta with chilli and bacon

450g (14 oz) spaghetti
1 tablespoon olive oil
2 red chillies, seeded and chopped
6 rashers bacon, rind removed, chopped
3/4 cup (6 fl oz) mascarpone*
1/2 cup shredded fresh basil
cracked black pepper
parmesan cheese, to serve

Place the spaghetti in a large saucepan of rapidly boiling
water and cook for 10 minutes or until al dente.
While the pasta is cooking, heat a frying pan over medium–
high heat. Add the olive oil, chillies and bacon and cook
for 4 minutes or until the bacon is crisp.
Drain the pasta and return it to the hot saucepan. Place
over low heat and add the chilli and bacon mixture together
with the mascarpone, basil and pepper. Mix to combine.
Serve topped with grated parmesan cheese. Serves 4.

green chilli chicken curry

3 green chillies, seeded and chopped
1 cup fresh coriander (cilantro) leaves
1 tablespoon fish sauce*
2 teaspoons ground cumin
1 tablespoon finely chopped ginger
1 red onion, chopped
2 tablespoons peanut oil
500g (1 lb) chicken thigh fillets, diced
250g (8 oz) new potatoes, halved
1 cup (8 fl oz) chicken stock
1 1/2 cups (12 fl oz) coconut milk
3 kaffir lime leaves, lightly crushed

Place the chillies, coriander, fish sauce, cumin, ginger,
onion and peanut oil in a food processor and process
until smooth. Heat a frying pan over medium heat and
add this spice paste. Cook, stirring, for 5 minutes or until
the paste is fragrant.
Add the chicken to the pan and cook, stirring to coat,
for 2 minutes. Add the potatoes, chicken stock, coconut
milk and kaffir lime leaves and simmer for 25 minutes or
until the chicken is tender and the curry is thick. Remove
the lime leaves and serve with basmati rice. Serves 4.

78

pasta with chilli and bacon

green chilli chicken curry

chilli tofu in coconut broth

roast tomato, chilli and balsamic relish

chicken salad with chilli–coconut milk dressing

chilli tofu in coconut broth

2 red chillies, seeded and chopped
3 tablespoons soy sauce
1 tablespoon grated ginger
2 tablespoons sugar
2 tablespoons lime juice
600g (1 1/4 lb) silken tofu, drained and chopped
1/3 cup fresh Thai basil leaves
coconut broth
2 1/2 cups (20 fl oz) coconut milk
2 1/2 cups (20 fl oz) vegetable stock
4 kaffir lime leaves, shredded
500g (1 lb) sweet potato, peeled and sliced
500g (1 lb) Chinese broccoli* (gai larn), halved

To make the coconut broth, place the coconut milk, vegetable stock and lime leaves in a deep frying pan over medium heat. Add the sweet potato and cook, covered, for 8 minutes. Add the Chinese broccoli and cook for a further 4 minutes.
To cook the tofu, place the chillies, soy sauce, ginger, sugar and lime juice in a frying pan over medium heat and allow to cook for 3 minutes. Add the tofu to the pan and cook for 1 minute each side or until coated with the chilli sauce.
To serve, place the coconut broth, sweet potato and Chinese broccoli into bowls. Top with the chilli tofu, sprinkle with basil leaves and serve. Serves 4.

roast tomato, chilli and balsamic relish

8 tomatoes, halved
2 tablespoons olive oil
3 tablespoons balsamic vinegar
cracked black pepper
1 tablespoon olive oil, extra
1 onion, chopped
3–4 red chillies, seeded and chopped
1/2 cup (4 fl oz) balsamic vinegar, extra
2 tablespoons brown sugar
sea salt to taste

Preheat the oven to 200°C (400°F). Place the tomatoes on a baking tray, flesh-side up, drizzle with olive oil and balsamic vinegar and sprinkle with black pepper. Bake for 30 minutes or until the tomatoes are soft. Roughly chop. Heat the extra oil in a frying pan over medium heat. Add the onion and chillies and cook for 3 minutes or until soft. Then add the tomatoes with their baking juices, the extra balsamic vinegar, the brown sugar and the sea salt and simmer for 15 minutes or until thick.
Serve the relish as a condiment to steaks, burgers, sandwiches or roasted meats. Store in sterilised jars* in the refrigerator for up to 3 months. Makes 4 cups.

chicken salad with chilli-coconut milk dressing

1 tablespoon peanut oil
2 red chillies, seeded and chopped
2 teaspoons grated lime rind
1 tablespoon sugar
4 chicken breast fillets
100g (3 1/2 oz) baby English spinach leaves
300g (10 oz) snake beans, trimmed and blanched
chilli–coconut milk dressing
1 red chilli, seeded and chopped
1/2 cup (4 fl oz) coconut milk
1/4 cup chopped fresh coriander (cilantro) leaves
3 tablespoons lime juice
1 tablespoon fish sauce*

Heat the oil in a frying pan over medium–high heat. Add the chillies, lime rind and sugar to the pan and cook for 1 minute. Add the chicken fillets and cook for 3 minutes each side or until golden. Set aside.
To make the chilli–coconut milk dressing, place the chilli, coconut milk, coriander, lime juice and fish sauce in a bowl and mix to combine.
To serve, place the spinach leaves and snake beans on serving plates. Slice the chicken thickly and place on the beans. Spoon over the dressing and serve. Serves 4.

chilli rice paper rolls

1 tablespoon peanut oil
2 tablespoons shredded ginger
5 large (mild) red chillies, seeded and shredded
2 kaffir lime leaves, shredded
300g (10 oz) peeled small green (raw) prawns
4 spring (green) onions, shredded
2 Lebanese cucumbers, shredded
1/3 cup shredded fresh mint
2 tablespoons lime juice
1 tablespoon fish sauce*
12 medium rice paper wrappers*

Heat the oil in a frying pan over medium heat. Add the ginger and chilli and cook for 3 minutes or until crisp. Add the kaffir lime leaves and prawns and cook for a further 3 minutes or until the prawns are cooked through. Set aside to cool. When cool, combine with the spring onions, cucumber, mint, lime juice and fish sauce.
Place a rice paper wrapper in a bowl of warm water for 30 seconds or until soft and pliable. Remove and pat dry. Place a little of the chilli salad down the centre of the rice paper wrapper and fold over one end to make a base. Roll over one side and then the other to enclose the filling. Serve the rice paper rolls with soy sauce or sweet chilli sauce in small bowls for dipping. Serves 4 as a starter

chilli rice paper rolls

5

garlic +onion

basics

Garlic, onions and other members of the *Allium* genus are some of the most pungent of all vegetables. Their powerful bite and odour are caused by a reaction between sulphur compounds and enzymes which are activated by the air when the bulbs are crushed or cut. Garlic and onions are integral to nearly all stocks, soups and stews.

Garlic is credited with medicinal and even religious virtues, but it is for its versatility in cooking that it is most well known. Used whole, chopped or crushed, raw, sautéed or roasted, garlic imparts a distinctive flavour that can vary from pungent to sweet. Garlic needs to be dried thoroughly before being stored or sold.

The onion is native to Asia and has been eaten and cultivated since prehistoric times. Onions can be divided into two groups: dry onions, which are left in the ground to mature, and green onions, which are pulled while still young and before the bulb has had a chance to fully form. The dry onions most commonly available are white, red, brown, pickling onions and shallots. Green onions are variously called spring onions, scallions and salad onions.

brown onions

These are readily available all year round. These mature onions have a firm, crackling golden-brown skin that needs to be peeled away before slicing or chopping the flesh. These are a great all-purpose cooking onion for roasting, frying or barbecuing. Store them in a cool, dry, well-ventilated place.

garlic

Garlic grows underground as a bulb consisting of numerous cloves, each of which is encased in a thin, papery skin. The smell of garlic only emerges once the cloves are cut, causing damage to the cell walls. The more you cut the cloves, the stronger the smell. Cooking the garlic, however, destroys the compound and therefore the garlic becomes much milder and sweeter. When choosing a head of garlic, make sure it is firm and dry without any soft or discoloured patches.

white onions

These are more pungent than brown onions and have a firm, papery white skin. Because of their pungency they are more likely to affect the eyes when chopping. This can be remedied by peeling them under water, or—the easiest way—just by being quick when peeling and chopping them. A well-ventilated kitchen also helps. White onions are a good all-round cooking onion.

spring onions

Also known as scallions, green onions, salad onions or shallots, these are immature onions pulled when the tops are still green and before the bulbs have swollen greatly. The tops are hollow and are used in addition to the white bulb end. These onions are used both raw and cooked and are best kept wrapped in a damp cloth in the refrigerator.

red onions

Some varieties of red onion are pungent, others are mild and sweet. Sometimes the red pigment may stop after the first layer, while in others it may penetrate right to the centre. Red onions make great salad or salsa onions and are equally good cooked. Choose firm, red onions with dry skins.

leek

The edible parts of the leek are the thick white stem and the palest part of the green tops. Remove the tough outer layers then clean between the leaves of the leeks by making a deep slit in the top and fanning out the leaves so that running water can remove the dirt and grit between the layers. Store leeks in the refrigerator.

leek

white onion

red onion

brown onion

spring onions

garlic

good ideas

garlic mayonnaise

Use homemade mayonnaise or a good-quality prepared mayonnaise. Add a couple of cloves of crushed garlic and a sprinkle of sea salt and pepper. This mayo is great served with fish, meats or on sandwiches. Substitute roasted garlic for raw garlic if you prefer a more mellow flavour.

roast garlic

Cut the tops from a few heads of garlic, drizzle with olive oil and roast in a 180°C (350°F) oven for 30 minutes or until soft. Cook the garlic when roasting any sort of meat; it tastes great popped from its skin and spread on top.

onions in their skins

Roast whole onions in their skins at 180°C (350°F) for around 1 hour or until soft. Cool and then squeeze the flesh from its skin. Use as the base for onion soup or as an onion purée for mixing with mashed potato.

a baking rack

Use leeks as a roasting rack for chicken, fish or meats. Place the leeks in the bottom of a baking dish with a little stock or water. Top with the meat or fish and roast until the meat is tender. Serve the leek-flavoured meat with the leeks.

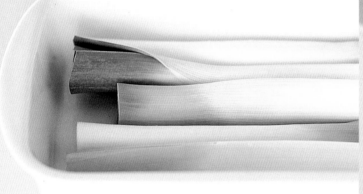

pickled onions

Peel small onions, place them in a saucepan and cover with white wine vinegar. Add a few bay leaves, some sprigs of herbs, peppercorns and sugar to taste. Simmer until soft, then place in sterilised jars*. Serve slices on sandwiches with meat, or as part of an antipasto plate.

caramelised onions

Place 8 sliced onions in a large frying pan with 3 tablespoons of oil and a sprinkle of sea salt and pepper. Cook over low heat, stirring occasionally and allowing the natural sugars in the onions to develop and sweeten. Serve warm or cold.

white bean dip

Place 1 drained can of cannellini beans, the cloves from 1 head of roasted garlic, 1/4 cup of chopped mint, 2 tablespoons of both lemon juice and olive oil and 1 teaspoon of ground cumin in a food processor and process until smooth. Drizzle with olive oil and serve with pita or Lebanese bread.

roast onion and garlic soup

onion and blue cheese tart

garlic roast pork with mash

roast onion and garlic soup

3 unpeeled heads garlic
8 brown onions, unpeeled, halved
3 tablespoons olive oil
2 cups (16 fl oz) water
4 cups (32 fl oz) beef stock
3 potatoes, peeled and chopped
2 tablespoons fresh thyme
cracked black pepper
parmesan cheese, to serve

Preheat the oven to 200°C (400°F). Place the garlic and onions on a baking tray, cut-side up, and drizzle with olive oil. Turn the onions on the tray so they are cut-side down. Bake for 50 minutes or until the garlic and onions are soft. Remove the onions and garlic from their skins and cut the onion flesh in half. Place in a large saucepan with the water, beef stock, potatoes, thyme and pepper. Cook over medium heat for 20 minutes or until the soup has thickened slightly. Serve in bowls sprinkled with parmesan and accompanied by slices of toasted bread. Serves 4.

onion and blue cheese tart

300g (10 oz) ready-prepared puff pastry
filling
2 tablespoons olive oil
4 brown onions, sliced
1 teaspoon grated lemon rind
200g (6½ oz) soft bitey blue cheese, crumbled
85g (3 oz) small olives
2 tablespoons fresh thyme
cracked black pepper

Preheat the oven to 200°C (400°F). Roll out the pastry on a lightly floured surface until it is a rough rectangular shape and 3mm (⅛ inch) thick. Line a baking tray with non-stick baking paper and place the pastry on the tray.
To make the filling, place the oil, onions and grated lemon rind in a frying pan over medium heat. Cook, stirring occasionally, for around 20 minutes or until the onions are soft and golden. Allow to cool slightly.
Sprinkle the blue cheese over the pastry, leaving a 2cm (¾ inch) border. Top with the onions, olives, thyme and pepper. Bake for 25–30 minutes or until the pastry is puffed and golden. To serve, slice the tart and serve warm with cress leaves. Serves 8 as a starter or 4 as a main.

garlic roast pork with mash

6-rib rack of pork loin
2 unpeeled heads garlic
4 cloves garlic, extra
olive oil and sea salt, for rubbing
garlic mash
5 potatoes, whole and unpeeled
60g (2 oz) butter
½ cup (4 fl oz) milk or cream
sea salt

Preheat the oven to 230°C (450°F). Make slits between the pork flesh and the bones and place the rack of meat, skin-side up, in a baking dish with the heads of garlic. Cut the extra cloves of garlic into pieces and place them into the slits made in the pork. Rub oil and sea salt into the pork skin and place in the oven. Bake for 25 minutes or until the skin is crisp and golden. Remove the garlic heads, reserving them for the mash, and reduce the oven to 180°C (350°F). Cook the pork for 25–35 minutes longer, or until cooked to your liking.
To make the garlic mash, place the potatoes in a saucepan of boiling water. Cook for 12 minutes or until soft. Drain and slip the skins from the potatoes. Place the potatoes back into the saucepan and return to the warm stovetop. Squeeze the garlic from the skins and mash together with the potatoes, adding the butter and milk or cream to form a smooth mash. Add salt and cover to keep warm.
To serve, slice the pork into thick pieces. Place the garlic mash onto serving plates and top with the pork. Serve with buttered steamed greens and fried apple slices. Serves 4.

pasta with garlic and parmesan spinach

450g (14 oz) spaghetti
3 tablespoons olive oil
4 cloves garlic, sliced
2 red chillies, seeded and chopped
2 tablespoons fresh oregano
½ teaspoon cracked black pepper
200g (6½ oz) baby English spinach leaves
¾ cup grated parmesan cheese
sea salt and extra cracked black pepper

Place the spaghetti in a large saucepan of rapidly boiling water and cook for 10–12 minutes or until al dente. While the pasta is cooking, heat the oil in a small saucepan over medium–low heat. Add the garlic, chilli, oregano and pepper and cook for 3 minutes or until the garlic is soft. Drain the pasta and place in a serving bowl. Pour over the garlic and oil mixture and add the spinach leaves, parmesan cheese, sea salt and extra pepper. Toss well to combine, and serve. Serves 4.

pasta with garlic and parmesan spinach

chicken roasted on potatoes and garlic

2 tablespoons olive oil
6 potatoes, peeled and chopped
1/4 cup fresh oregano
12 cloves garlic, unpeeled
sea salt and cracked black pepper
4 chicken breast fillets, skin on
oil, for brushing

Preheat the oven to 200°C (400°F). Place the oil, potatoes, oregano, garlic, salt and pepper in a baking dish and toss to combine. Bake for 25–30 minutes or until the potatoes are almost cooked.

While the potatoes are cooking, brush the chicken fillets with a little oil and sprinkle the skin with extra salt and pepper. Heat a frying pan over medium–high heat. Add the chicken to the pan, skin-side down, and cook for 3 minutes or until the skin is well browned. Then place the chicken, skin-side up, on top of the potatoes and garlic in the baking dish. Bake for a further 10 minutes or until the chicken is cooked through.

To serve, place the chicken and potatoes on serving plates. Squeeze the garlic from its skin and spread on the potatoes and chicken. Serve with steamed beans and a squeeze of lemon. Serves 4.

roasted vegetable salad with garlic dressing

8 small wedges pumpkin
650g (1 lb 5 oz) orange sweet potato (kumera), peeled and chopped
2 parsnips, peeled and halved
2 baby fennel bulbs, halved
2 unpeeled heads garlic
olive oil, for drizzling
sea salt and cracked black pepper
garlic dressing
2 tablespoons cider vinegar
3 tablespoons olive oil
2 tablespoons grated parmesan cheese

Preheat the oven to 200°C (400°F). Place the pumpkin, sweet potato, parsnip, fennel and garlic in a baking dish. Drizzle with olive oil and sprinkle with salt and pepper. Bake for 35 minutes or until the vegetables are golden and soft. Remove the garlic from the dish, then turn off the oven but leave the vegetables in there to keep warm. To make the garlic dressing, squeeze the garlic from its skin and place in a blender or food processor. Add the vinegar, olive oil and parmesan and blend until smooth. To serve, spoon the garlic dressing over the roasted vegetables. Serves 4.

chicken roasted on potatoes and garlic

roasted vegetable salad with garlic dressing

onion marmalade

8 brown onions, sliced
1 tablespoon cumin seeds
1 tablespoon coriander seeds
3 cups (24 fl oz) white wine vinegar
2½ cups (20 fl oz) light brown sugar

Place the onions, cumin seeds, coriander seeds and vinegar in a saucepan over medium–high heat. Cover and allow to rapidly simmer for 15 minutes. Add the brown sugar to the pan and cook, uncovered, for 1 hour or until the onions are soft and the syrup is thick. Pour into sterilised jars* and seal immediately.
Serve the onion marmalade on sandwiches with roasted vegetables or meat. Makes 5 cups.
note – This marmalade can be kept sealed for up to 1 year. After opening, store in the refrigerator for up to 8 weeks.

leek risotto with lemon fish

5 cups (40 fl oz) vegetable stock
2 tablespoons olive oil
3 leeks, sliced
2 cups arborio* or risotto rice
½ cup shaved or grated parmesan cheese
2 tablespoons lemon juice
cracked black pepper
lemon fish
60g (2 oz) butter
2 teaspoons shredded lemon rind
2 tablespoons chopped fresh flat-leaf parsley
4 x 180g (6 oz) firm white fish fillets
2 tablespoons lemon juice

To make the risotto, place the vegetable stock in a saucepan over medium heat and bring to a slow simmer. Place the olive oil in a heavy-based saucepan, add the leeks and cook for 6 minutes or until golden. Add the rice to the pan and stir for 1 minute or until translucent. Slowly add 1 cup of the hot stock to the rice and stir constantly until the liquid has been absorbed. Repeat with cups of the stock, only adding more when all the liquid has been absorbed. Continue adding stock until the rice is soft and creamy. If you need more liquid, heat extra stock or water. To make the lemon fish, heat the butter, lemon rind and parsley in a frying pan over medium–high heat. Cut each fish fillet in half and add to the pan. Cook for 2 minutes each side or until tender, then pour over the lemon juice. Stir the parmesan, lemon juice and pepper through the risotto and serve in bowls, topped with the fish. Serve with lemon wedges and extra parmesan cheese. Serves 4.

prawn, leek and spinach linguine

450g (14 oz) linguine*
2 tablespoons olive oil
4 leeks, cut into long strips
1kg (2 lb) medium green (raw) prawns, peeled
⅓ cup salted capers*, rinsed
3 tablespoons lemon juice
1 tablespoon grated lemon rind
90g (3 oz) baby English spinach leaves
cracked black pepper

Place the linguini in a large saucepan of rapidly boiling water and cook until al dente.
While the pasta is cooking, place the olive oil in a frying pan over medium–high heat. Add the leeks and cook for 5 minutes or until golden. Add the prawns and cook, stirring, for 2 minutes. Add the capers, lemon juice and lemon rind and cook for a further 2 minutes or until the prawns are cooked.
Drain the linguini and place in a large serving bowl with the spinach leaves. Add the prawn mixture, sprinkle with cracked black pepper and toss well to combine. Serve immediately. Serves 4.

onion-simmered shanks

2 tablespoons olive oil
1.5kg (3 lb) veal shank, cut into 8 thick slices
plain (all-purpose) flour, for dusting
1 tablespoon olive oil, extra
4 brown or white onions, sliced
3 cloves garlic, sliced
3 bay leaves
4 cups (32 fl oz) beef stock
1 cup (8 fl oz) dry white wine
⅓ cup (2¾ fl oz) lemon juice

Preheat the oven to 180°C (350°F). Heat the oil in a large frying pan over high heat. Coat the shanks in flour and add to the pan a few at a time, cooking for 4 minutes each side or until well browned. Place the shanks in a large baking dish.
Heat the extra oil in the frying pan and add the onions. Cook, stirring occasionally, for 8 minutes or until the onions are soft and golden. Add the garlic, bay leaves, beef stock, wine and lemon juice to the baking dish containing the shanks and cover with a lid or aluminium foil. Bake for 85 minutes, then turn the veal. Bake uncovered for a further 30 minutes or until the veal is soft. Serve on creamy mashed potato. Serves 4.

onion marmalade

prawn, leek and spinach linguine

leek risotto with lemon fish

onion-simmered shanks

bacon fritters with balsamic onions

simmered lentils with roasted leeks

seared beef and pickled red onion salad

bacon fritters with balsamic onions

1 cup self-raising (self-rising) flour
1/2 teaspoon baking powder
3 eggs
3/4 cup (6 fl oz) milk
85g (3 oz) butter, melted
8 rashers smoked bacon, rind and fat removed
1/2 cup grated cheddar cheese
sea salt and cracked black pepper
oil, for frying
100g (31/2 oz) baby English spinach leaves
balsamic onions
1 tablespoon olive oil
4 brown or red onions, cut into wedges
1/3 cup (23/4 fl oz) balsamic vinegar
3/4 cup (6 fl oz) chicken stock
2 tablespoons brown sugar
2 tablespoons fresh thyme

To make the balsamic onions, heat the oil in a saucepan over medium–low heat. Add the onions, vinegar, stock, sugar and thyme and cook, covered, stirring occasionally, for 30 minutes or until the onions are soft and golden. Make the bacon fritters while the onions are cooking. Place the flour and baking powder in a bowl. In another bowl, whisk together the eggs, milk and melted butter. Pour into the flour, stirring until smooth. Slice the bacon and add to the mixture, along with the cheese, salt and pepper. Heat a little oil in a frying pan over medium–low heat. Add 3–4 tablespoons of the fritter mixture and cook for 3 minutes each side or until puffed and golden. To serve, place the bacon fritters on serving plates and top with the spinach leaves and balsamic onions. Serve hot. Serves 4.

baked garlic borlotti beans

1 kg (2 lb) fresh borlotti beans in the pod
8 cloves peeled garlic
12 small spring (green) onions
6 very ripe tomatoes, halved
3 cups (24 fl oz) beef stock
8 sprigs fresh lemon thyme
2 tablespoons chopped fresh mint
sea salt and cracked black pepper

Preheat the oven to 200°C (400°F). Remove the beans from the pod and place in a baking dish. Add the garlic, spring onions, tomatoes, beef stock and lemon thyme. Cover tightly and bake for 1 hour.
Remove the cover and stir the beans. Bake uncovered for a further 20 minutes or until the beans are soft. Stir through the mint, sea salt and pepper. Serve the baked beans on wood-fired bread made into garlic bruschetta. Serves 4.

simmered lentils with roasted leeks

4 leeks, halved lengthways
4 tomatoes, halved
2 tablespoons olive oil
sea salt and cracked black pepper
simmered lentils
2 teaspoons olive oil
2 cloves garlic, sliced
315g (10 oz) du puy lentils*
33/4 cups (30 fl oz) vegetable stock
1/2 cup shredded fresh flat-leaf parsley
3 tablespoons lemon juice

Preheat the oven to 180°C (350°F). Place the leeks, cut-side up, on a baking tray and top with the tomatoes, also cut-side up. Drizzle with olive oil and sprinkle with salt and pepper. Bake for 40 minutes or until the leeks and tomatoes are soft.
To make the simmered lentils, place the oil in a frying pan over medium heat. Add the garlic and cook for 1 minute or until soft. Add the lentils and the stock and simmer, covered, for 35 minutes or until just tender.
To serve, place the leeks and tomatoes on serving plates. Stir the parsley, lemon juice and some salt and pepper through the lentils. Spoon over the leeks and tomatoes and serve. Serves 4.

seared beef and pickled red onion salad

650g (1 lb 5 oz) rump or sirloin steak
oil, for brushing
cracked black pepper
pickled red onion salad
2 red onions, finely chopped
3 spring (green) onions, shredded
1/2 cup (4 fl oz) cider vinegar
3 tablespoons sugar
1/2 cup roughly chopped fresh mint
1/4 cup chopped fresh flat-leaf parsley
150g (5 oz) baby English spinach leaves

To make the pickled red onion salad, place the red onions, spring onions, vinegar and sugar in a bowl and allow to stand for 10 minutes.
Meanwhile, brush both sides of the steak with oil and sprinkle with cracked black pepper. Preheat a frying pan or grill pan over high heat. Cook the steak for 2 minutes each side or until well seared and cooked to your liking.
Slice the steak into thick pieces. Toss the pickled red onion salad with the mint, parsley and spinach leaves and place on serving plates. Top with the seared steak pieces and serve. Serves 4.

baked garlic borlotti beans

balsamic chicken with garlic couscous

4 chicken breast fillets
1/3 cup (2¾ fl oz) balsamic vinegar
1/2 cup (4 fl oz) chicken stock
2 tablespoons sugar
1 clove garlic, crushed
garlic couscous
1½ cups couscous*
2¼ cups (18 fl oz) boiling chicken stock
60g (2 oz) butter
4 cloves garlic, sliced
2 tablespoons fresh thyme

Place the chicken fillets in a shallow dish and pour over the combined balsamic vinegar, chicken stock, sugar and garlic. Allow to marinate for 10 minutes each side.
To make the garlic couscous, place the couscous in a bowl and pour in the boiling stock. Cover tightly with plastic wrap and allow to stand for 5 minutes or until all the liquid has been absorbed. Heat the butter in a frying pan over medium–low heat. Add the garlic and thyme and cook for 3 minutes or until the garlic is soft but not brown. Add the couscous to the pan and cook, stirring, for 2 minutes.
To cook the chicken, preheat an oiled frying pan over medium–high heat. Remove the chicken from the marinade and add to the pan, cooking for 3–4 minutes each side. Add the marinade to the pan and cook the chicken for a further 1 minute each side or until the chicken is cooked through and the marinade has thickened.
To serve, place the couscous on serving plates and top with the chicken and pan sauce. Serve with steamed beans or other greens. Serves 4.

spring onion pancakes with hoisin chicken

1 cup plain (all-purpose) flour
1/2 cup rice flour
3 eggs
1½ cups (12 fl oz) milk
pinch sea salt
1 tablespoon sesame oil*
4 spring (green) onions, shredded
hoisin chicken
2/3 cup (5½ fl oz) hoisin sauce*
4 tablespoons soy sauce
2 tablespoons sugar
4 chicken breast fillets
6 spring (green) onions, shredded

To make the pancakes, place the plain flour, rice flour, eggs, milk, salt and sesame oil in a bowl and whisk until smooth. Stir through the spring onions. Grease a frying pan and place over medium–high heat. Pour in large spoonfuls of the pancake mixture and swirl the pan to spread the mixture thinly. Cook for 2 minutes each side or until lightly browned. Keep the pancakes warm.
To cook the hoisin chicken, heat a frying pan over medium heat, add the hoisin sauce, soy sauce and sugar to the pan and cook for 2 minutes. Add the chicken to the pan and cook for 5 minutes each side or until the chicken is cooked through and the sauce is thick.
To serve, slice the chicken into thin strips and place on top of the pancakes. Spoon over a little of the pan sauce and sprinkle with shredded spring onions. Fold over the pancake to enclose. Serve with steamed greens for a main meal. Serves 4

balsamic chicken with garlic couscous

spring onion pancakes with hoisin chicken

chocolate 6

basics

Chocolate is made by complex means. Over 30 different varieties of cocoa beans are available and so the producers of chocolate, much like the producers of coffee, are able to blend different beans to achieve the desired flavour.

The seeds of cocoa beans, which are the fruit of the cacao tree native to the rainforests of South America, are fermented to neutralise their bitterness, then dried and roasted to intensify the aroma and flavour. Next, the beans are cracked to reveal the kernel or 'nib'. This is heated and ground to release the highly prized cocoa liquor—the base of all chocolate. Cocoa liquor is further refined to extract cocoa butter and cocoa powder.

To make chocolate, cocoa liquor and cocoa butter are first kneaded together with sugar, milk products and various flavourings. This chocolate mass is then ground to a fine consistency before being churned to enrich the flavour and impart a smooth texture to the chocolate.

milk couverture chocolate

Couverture is a high-quality chocolate with a high cocoa butter content. Milk couverture is semi-sweet chocolate and contains milk in a dried or concentrated form. The milk in this chocolate makes it difficult to use for cooking and baking, as it cannot take even moderate heat without burning. It can, however, be used successfully in mousses and glazes that only require minimal heat. Milk chocolate doesn't store very well: keep it well wrapped to avoid it absorbing moisture and odours from the air.

dark couverture chocolate

This ranges from bitter or unsweetened dark chocolate containing 66% cocoa, to semi-sweet dark chocolate containing 55% cocoa and a small quantity of sugar. Bitter or unsweetened chocolate contains pure cocoa particles. This chocolate needs sweetening when using in baking. Semi-sweet dark couverture is great for cooking with or melting to shape, as well as for coating and piping. It needs to be tempered* before moulding or coating. Dark chocolate has good keeping qualities. It can be stored, well wrapped, in a cool, dry place for a year or longer.

white chocolate

This is the chocolate impostor. White chocolate doesn't actually contain any chocolate liquor. The best white chocolates are ivory or cream coloured, never completely white. Good white chocolate doesn't tolerate heat and should never be substituted for dark chocolate. White chocolate has a short shelf life. To store it, wrap well and keep in the freezer.

cocoa powder

After the extraction of cocoa butter and liquor, the solid mass of the cocoa bean remains in the press. This is pulverised to make a powder called cocoa. Cocoa contains between 10% and 24% cocoa butter and no sugar. Two types of cocoa are available: natural or non-alkalised, and alkalised. Cocoa that has been alkalised has a low acidity and a rich colour and flavour. This quality cocoa powder is ideal for cooking. When cooking, do not substitute sweetened cocoas or hot chocolate mixes for cocoa.

compound chocolate

Compound chocolate is an inferior chocolate to couverture, but it is very easy to use. It doesn't burn as easily as real chocolate because most, if not all, of the cocoa butter has been replaced by palm oil, soybean oil and emulsifiers. This chocolate is good for coating or decorating as it doesn't need to be tempered.

milk couverture chocolate

cocoa powder

dark couverture chocolate

compound chocolate

white chocolate

107

good ideas

giant chocolate sparkles

Spoon melted chocolate into large, thin rounds onto non-stick baking paper. Leave for 3 minutes or until just beginning to set, then sprinkle with silver sugar sprinkles. Refrigerate until set.

chocolate liqueur

Melt 125g (4 oz) of chopped milk chocolate and 1 cup (8 fl oz) of cream over low heat until smooth. Cool. Stir through 3–4 tablespoons of nut liqueur. Serve neat or over ice. Store in the refrigerator for up to 2 weeks.

chocolate ice cream bites

These are the perfect way to finish a meal. Place small balls of ice cream on chilled trays and leave in the freezer until firm. Dip into slightly cooled melted chocolate and freeze to set.

white chocolate milk

Finely chop white chocolate and place it in the bottom of a tall, thick glass. Top with hot milk and stir until the chocolate dissolves. Serve with a long spoon.

chocolate brownie sundae

For a true chocolate feast, top a large square of chocolate brownie with scoops of your favourite ice cream and then drizzle with chocolate sauce.

chocolate truffles

Gently heat 250g (8 oz) of chocolate, 55g (2 oz) of butter and 2/3 cup (5 1/2 fl oz) of cream and mix until smooth. Cool in the refrigerator then shape into small balls. Toss in cocoa to serve.

chocolate mirror glaze

Make a shiny glaze for any cake by adding 1 tablespoon of vegetable oil to 300g (10 oz) of dark chocolate. Heat until smooth. Chill the cake well before pouring over the glaze.

chocolate berry ice cream cakes   chocolate cookies

simple chocolate pound cake with chocolate glaze

chocolate berry ice cream cakes

1 quantity simple chocolate pound cake (see opposite)
350g (11 oz) mixed fresh or frozen berries
1 litre (32 fl oz) quality vanilla or chocolate ice cream, softened

Bake the chocolate pound cake in a 23cm (9 inch) square cake tin. Cool the cake and cut in half horizontally.
Mix the berries and the softened ice cream until just combined. Place this berry and ice cream mixture into a lined 23cm (9 inch) square cake tin and freeze for 1 hour or until firm.
Remove the ice cream from the tin. Place a layer of chocolate cake on a serving plate, top with the ice cream and then with the remaining layer of cake.
To serve, cut the cake into small sandwiches with a serrated knife. Serve immediately. Serves 12.

chocolate cookies

250g (8 oz) butter, softened
1 teaspoon vanilla extract
1½ cups brown sugar
2 eggs
1 cup plain (all-purpose) flour
1 cup self-raising (self-rising) flour
½ cup cocoa powder
½ cup desiccated coconut
250g (8 oz) chopped dark chocolate

Preheat the oven to 160°C (315°F). Place the butter, vanilla and sugar in the bowl of an electric mixer and beat until creamy. Beat in the eggs and then stir through the flours, cocoa, coconut and chocolate.
Place level ¼ cupfuls of the mixture on baking trays lined with non-stick baking paper and bake for 12–15 minutes or until the bases are lightly browned.
Serve the cookies warm or cold with hot chocolate. Makes 18.

simple chocolate pound cake with chocolate glaze

250g (8 oz) unsalted butter, softened
1 cup caster (superfine) sugar
6 large eggs
1½ cups plain (all-purpose) flour
½ teaspoon baking powder
¾ cup cocoa powder
chocolate glaze
185g (6 oz) dark chocolate, chopped
½ cup (4 fl oz) cream

Preheat the oven to 180°C (350°F). Place the butter and sugar in the bowl of an electric mixer and beat until light and creamy. Add the eggs one at a time and beat well. Sift the flour, baking powder and cocoa over the butter mixture and stir to combine.
Pour the mixture into a 20cm (8 inch) square cake tin that has been lined with non-stick baking paper. Bake for 40 minutes or until cooked when tested with a skewer. Cool on a wire rack.
To make the glaze, place the chocolate and cream in a saucepan and stir until melted and smooth. Set aside to cool at room temperature.
To finish, place the cake in the refrigerator and chill for 30 minutes. Pour the cooled glaze over the cake and then refrigerate to set. Serves 8.

chocolate macaroon sandwiches

3 egg whites
¾ cup sugar
3 cups desiccated coconut
chocolate filling
¼ cup (2 fl oz) cream
90g (3 oz) dark couverture chocolate, chopped
30g (1 oz) butter

Preheat the oven to 180°C (350°F). Place the egg whites, sugar and coconut in a bowl and mix to combine.
Press single tablespoons of this macaroon mixture into flat balls and place on baking trays lined with non-stick baking paper. Bake for 10 minutes or until just golden. Cool on the trays.
To make the chocolate filling, place the cream in a saucepan over medium heat and bring almost to the boil. Remove from the heat, add the chocolate and butter and stir until smooth. Refrigerate until cold and thick.
To assemble, spread a macaroon with the chocolate filling and then sandwich with another macaroon.
These are great to serve with strong coffee. Makes 16.

chocolate macaroon sandwiches

chocolate brownies

250g (8 oz) butter
1 teaspoon vanilla extract
1½ cups sugar
¼ cup brown sugar
4 eggs
1⅓ cups plain (all-purpose) flour
¾ cup cocoa powder
¼ teaspoon baking powder

Preheat the oven to 170°C (325°F). Place the butter, vanilla, sugar and brown sugar in the bowl of an electric mixer and beat until light and fluffy. Add the eggs one at a time and beat well.
Sift the flour, cocoa and baking powder over the butter mixture and fold through.
Pour the mixture into a 20cm (8 inch) square cake tin, base-lined with non-stick baking paper, and bake for 40–50 minutes or until set. Cool in the tin. Cut into squares and serve warm or cool with espresso coffee or icy-cold milk. Makes 16 pieces.

triple-choc brownies

185g (6 oz) butter
185g (6 oz) dark chocolate, chopped
3 eggs
1¼ cups caster (superfine) sugar
⅔ cup plain (all-purpose) flour
½ cup cocoa powder
¾ cup roughly chopped white chocolate
¾ cup roughly chopped milk chocolate

Preheat the oven to 180°C (350°F). Place the butter and dark chocolate in a saucepan over low heat and stir until just smooth. Allow to cool. Place the eggs and sugar in the bowl of an electric mixer and beat until light and creamy. Fold through the chocolate and butter mixture. Sift the flour and cocoa over the mixture and mix to combine. Add the white and milk chocolate then pour into a 23cm (9 inch) square cake tin, base-lined with non-stick baking paper. Bake for 35–40 minutes or until set. Allow to cool, then cut into squares. For a total indulgence, serve with a glass of liqueur. Makes 20 pieces.

rum and raisin brownies

¾ cup raisins
½ cup (4 fl oz) dark rum
200g (6½ oz) butter
125g (4 oz) dark chocolate, chopped
2 cups sugar
4 eggs
1 cup plain (all-purpose) flour
2 tablespoons cocoa powder
¼ teaspoon baking powder

Preheat the oven to 180°C (350°F). Place the raisins and rum in a saucepan over low heat and simmer until almost all of the rum has been absorbed. Set aside to cool. Place the butter and chocolate in a saucepan over low heat and stir until smooth. Place the chocolate mixture in a bowl and add the sugar, eggs, flour, cocoa, baking powder and raisins and mix until combined.
Pour the mixture into a 20cm (8 inch) square cake tin that has been side- and base-lined with non-stick baking paper. Bake for 50–60 minutes or until set. Cool completely before cutting into squares to serve. Makes 24 pieces.

nut brownies

200g (6½ oz) dark chocolate, chopped
250g (8 oz) butter
1¾ cups brown sugar
4 eggs
1 cup plain (all-purpose) flour
¼ teaspoon baking powder
⅓ cup cocoa powder
100g (3½ oz) macadamia nuts, roughly chopped
100g (3½ oz) toasted hazelnuts, roughly chopped

Preheat the oven to 180°C (350°F). Place the chocolate and butter in a saucepan over low heat and stir until smooth. Place the sugar, eggs, flour, baking powder, cocoa and the chocolate mixture into a bowl and mix to combine. Stir through the macadamia nuts and hazelnuts and then pour the mixture into a 23cm (9 inch) square cake tin, base-lined with non-stick baking paper. Bake for 30–35 minutes or until set. Cool in the tin and serve in small squares. Makes 24 pieces.

chocolate brownies

rum and raisin brownies

triple-choc brownies

nut brownies

layered chocolate fudge cake

75g (2½ oz) butter
1 teaspoon vanilla extract
8 eggs
1⅓ cups sugar
⅔ cup cocoa powder
1 cup plain (all-purpose) flour
fudge filling
375g (12 oz) dark couverture chocolate, chopped
¾ cup (6 fl oz) cream
155g (5 oz) butter

Preheat the oven to 180°C (350°F). Line the bases of two 20cm (8 inch) round cake tins with non-stick baking paper. Melt the butter and vanilla in a saucepan over low heat, then set aside to cool slightly.
Place the eggs and sugar in the bowl of an electric mixer and beat for 8 minutes or until the mixture is light and creamy and tripled in bulk.
Sift the cocoa and flour twice, then sift over the egg mixture and fold gently with the butter mixture until just combined. Divide the mixture between the cake tins.
Bake for 25 minutes or until the cakes shrink away from the sides of their tins. Cool in the tins. Cut each cake into two layers.
To make the fudge filling, place the chocolate, cream and butter in a saucepan over low heat and stir until smooth. Remove from the heat and refrigerate until cool, then place the fudge filling in the bowl of an electric mixer and beat until light and fluffy.
To assemble, place one layer of cake on a serving plate and spread with the filling. Repeat with remaining cake layers and the remaining fudge filling. Serves 10–12.

chocolate sorbet

2¾ cups (22 fl oz) water
1 cup sugar
1 cup cocoa powder

Place the water and sugar in a saucepan over low heat and stir until the sugar has dissolved. Add the cocoa powder and allow the syrup to simmer for 15 minutes. Remove from the heat and cool.
Pour the mixture into an ice cream maker and follow the manufacturer's instructions until the sorbet is frozen and scoopable. Alternatively, place the mixture in a metal container and freeze, beating at 1-hour intervals, until the sorbet is smooth and scoopable. Serves 4–6.

chocolate pear cake

80g (2¾ oz) butter
⅔ cup brown sugar
2 tablespoons water
4 small small pears, peeled, halved and cored
cake
185g (6 oz) butter
1½ cups brown sugar
3 eggs
2 cups self-raising (self-rising) flour
⅓ cup cocoa powder

Preheat the oven to 180°C (350°F). Place the butter, sugar and water in a frying pan over medium heat and stir until the butter has melted. Add the pears to the pan, cut-side down, and cook for 2 minutes.
Place the pears, cut-side down, in a 23cm (9 inch) round cake tin that has been side- and base-lined with non-stick baking paper. Pour over the pan juices and set aside.
To make the cake, place the butter and brown sugar in the bowl of an electric mixer and beat until light and fluffy. Add the eggs one at a time and beat well. Sift the flour and cocoa over the mixture and stir through.
Spoon the mixture over the pears in the tin. Bake for 50–60 minutes or until cooked when tested with a skewer. Cool in the tin for 5 minutes, then invert onto a serving plate and serve the cake in wedges with cream. Serves 8–10.

liqueur chocolate cake

125g (4 oz) dark couverture chocolate, chopped
155g (5 oz) butter
3 eggs
⅓ cup caster (superfine) sugar
⅓ cup plain (all-purpose) flour
⅓ cup self-raising (self-rising) flour
1 cup almond meal (ground almonds)
⅓ cup (2¾ fl oz) liqueur such as Frangelico, Amaretto or Grand Marnier

Preheat the oven to 160°C (315°F). Place the chocolate and butter in a saucepan over low heat and stir until smooth. Place the eggs, sugar, flours, almonds, liqueur and chocolate mixture in a bowl and mix to combine.
Pour the mixture into a 20cm (8 inch) round cake tin that has been base-lined with non-stick baking paper. Bake for 30 minutes or until cooked when tested with a skewer. Serve warm in slices with a glass of liqueur. Serves 10–12.

layered chocolate fudge cake

chocolate pear cake

chocolate sorbet

liqueur chocolate cake

malted chocolate puddings

chocolate panna cotta

malted chocolate puddings

185g (6 oz) dark chocolate, chopped
185g (6 oz) butter
1/2 cup malted milk powder
4 eggs, separated
1/2 cup sugar
1/2 cup almond meal (ground almonds)
1/3 cup plain (all-purpose) flour
3 tablespoons sugar, extra

Preheat the oven to oven 160°C (315°F). Place the chocolate, butter and malted milk powder in a saucepan over very low heat and stir until melted and smooth. Remove from the heat and set aside.

Place the egg yolks and sugar in a bowl and beat until light and creamy. Fold the chocolate mixture, the almonds and the flour through the egg yolks.

Place the egg whites in a bowl and beat until soft peaks form. While beating, gradually add the extra sugar until the mixture is glossy. Fold this egg white mixture through the chocolate mixture.

Pour the mixture into six greased 1-cup (8 fl oz) capacity teacups or dariole moulds. Place on a baking tray and pour enough hot water into the tray to come halfway up the sides of the cups. Bake for 25 minutes or until the edges are cooked but the centres are a little soft.

Serve in tea cups or unmould and serve with thick cream. Serves 6.

chocolate panna cotta

4 cups (32 fl oz) cream
3/4 cup icing (confectioners') sugar
1 teaspoon vanilla extract
185g (6 oz) milk or dark couverture chocolate, chopped
2 teaspoons gelatine
1/4 cup (2 fl oz) water

Place the cream, icing sugar and vanilla in a saucepan and allow to slowly simmer, stirring occasionally until the liquid has reduced by a third. Be sure the cream doesn't catch on the bottom of the pan. Add the chocolate and stir until smooth.

Place the gelatine in a bowl and add the water. Leave for 5 minutes. Place the gelatine mixture in a saucepan over low heat until the gelatine has dissolved. Stir into the hot cream and chocolate mixture and simmer for 1 minute. Pour into six 1/2-cup (4 fl oz) capacity moulds or ramekins and refrigerate for 4–6 hours or until firm. Serve with fruit. Serves 6.

muddy chocolate cake

chocolate-chip semi freddo

chocolate truffle cakes

muddy chocolate cake

300g (10 oz) dark couverture chocolate, chopped
250g (8 oz) butter
5 eggs, separated
1/4 cup caster (superfine) sugar
1 teaspoon vanilla extract
3/4 cup self-raising (self-rising) flour
berries, to serve

Preheat the oven to 130°C (260°F). Place the chocolate and butter in a saucepan and stir over low heat until melted and smooth. Set aside. Place the egg yolks, sugar and vanilla in the bowl of an electric mixer and beat until the mixture is thick and pale.
In a separate bowl, beat the egg whites until stiff peaks form. Fold the chocolate mixture into the egg yolk mixture, sift the flour over the top and gently fold through. Carefully fold the egg whites through the mixture and then pour into a 20cm (8 inch) round cake tin, base-lined with non-stick baking paper. Bake for 75 minutes or until the cake is firm. Cool in the tin.
Serve the cake with berries. Serves 8–10.
note – The flavour and texture of this cake are best when it is served at room temperature, not chilled.

chocolate-chip semi freddo

2 cups (16 fl oz) cream
1/3 cup sugar
1 teaspoon vanilla extract
4 eggs, separated
85g (3 oz) dark chocolate, grated
85g (3 oz) milk chocolate, grated

Place the cream in a bowl and whisk until firm. Refrigerate until required.
Place the sugar, vanilla and egg yolks in the bowl of an electric mixer and beat until the mixture is thick and pale. Place the egg whites in the bowl of an electric mixer and beat until soft peaks form. Gently fold together the cream, egg whites, egg yolk mixture and the grated dark and milk chocolate. Pour the mixture into a metal container and cover. Freeze for 3 hours or until firm. Serve in scoops. Serves 6.

chocolate truffle cakes

300g (10 oz) dark couverture chocolate, chopped
150g (5 oz) butter
6 eggs
1 teaspoon vanilla extract
4 tablespoons caster (superfine) sugar
chocolate glaze
200g (6½ oz) dark chocolate, chopped
1/3 cup (2¾ fl oz) cream
85g (3 oz) butter

Preheat the oven to 170°C (325°F). Line the base of eight 1-cup (8 fl oz) capacity non-stick muffin tins with non-stick baking paper.
Place the chocolate and butter in a saucepan and stir over low heat until melted and smooth.
Place the eggs, vanilla and sugar in the bowl of an electric mixer and beat until thick and pale. Stir through the chocolate mixture.
Spoon the mixture into the muffin tins and bake for 12–15 minutes or until the cakes are just set. Cool in the tins and then refrigerate for 2 hours.
To make the glaze, place the chocolate, cream and butter in a saucepan over low heat and mix until smooth. Chill the glaze until firm.
Unmould the cakes onto serving plates and spread with the glaze. Serves 8.

white chocolate tart

1 quantity sweet shortcrust pastry*, or 375g (12 oz)
   ready-prepared pastry
225g (7 oz) raspberries
filling
300g (10 oz) white chocolate, chopped
2 cups (16 fl oz) cream
4 egg yolks

Preheat the oven to 200°C (400°F). Roll the pastry out on a lightly floured surface until 3mm (1/8 inch) thick. Place the pastry in a 25cm (10 inch) removable-base tart tin. Prick the pastry with a fork and top with a piece of non-stick baking paper. Fill with baking weights or rice and bake for 5 minutes. Remove the weights and paper and cook for a further 6 minutes or until the pastry is a light golden colour.
To make the filling, place the chocolate and cream in a saucepan over low heat and stir until smooth. Remove the mixture from the heat and whisk in the egg yolks. Pour the mixture into the tart shell and bake at 140°C (275°F) for 25 minutes or until the tart is just set. Refrigerate until cold and firm. To serve, top with the raspberries and cut into thin wedges. Serves 12.

white chocolate tart

chocolate ice cream cones

½ cup (4 fl oz) milk
2 cups (16 fl oz) cream
185g (6 oz) dark couverture chocolate, chopped
5 egg yolks
½ cup caster (superfine) sugar

Place the milk, cream and chocolate in a saucepan and stir over low heat until smooth. Whisk in the egg yolks and sugar and stir until the mixture thickens slightly and coats the back of a spoon. Allow to cool.
Use 8 cone-shaped ice cream moulds or make cones from non-stick baking paper. Pour the mixture into the cones and stand in tall glasses so they stand straight. Freeze for 2–3 hours or until firm.
To serve, unmould or peel off the paper and place the ice cream cones on serving plates. Serves 8.

chocolate espresso syrup cake

300g (10 oz) dark chocolate, chopped
250g (8 oz) butter
5 eggs
4 tablespoons sugar
1 cup plain (all-purpose) flour
1 teaspoon baking powder
½ cup almond meal (ground almonds)
espresso syrup
¾ cup (6 fl oz) strong espresso coffee
¼ cup sugar

Preheat the oven to 160°C (315°F). Place the chocolate and butter in a saucepan over low heat and stir until smooth. Set aside.
Place the eggs and sugar in a bowl and beat until pale and thick. Sift the flour and baking powder over the egg mixture and gently fold through, then fold through the almonds and the chocolate mixture.
Pour the mixture into a 23cm (9 inch) round cake tin that has been base-lined with non-stick baking paper. Bake for 45 minutes or until cooked when tested with a skewer. While the cake is cooking, prepare the syrup. Place the espresso and sugar in a saucepan over medium heat and allow the syrup to simmer for 4 minutes. Pour half to three-quarters of the hot syrup over the cake in its tin. Invert the cake onto a plate and drizzle with the extra syrup. Serve warm. Serves 10.
note – If the coffee syrup is too bitter for your taste, add a little more sugar.

chocolate ice cream cones   chocolate espresso syrup cake

salt + pepper

7

basics

Salt and pepper are two of the most popular condiments in the world. Few tables don't carry twin cellars of these seasonings, and few savoury dishes are not enhanced by the addition of either salt or pepper.

Salt, a mineral consisting mainly of sodium chloride, brings out the flavour of many foods. If used in sufficient quantities, it can also preserve it. Dug from the earth or harvested from the sea, salt comes in a wide variety of forms: coarse crystals, delicate flakes or a crystalline powder.

Pepper was once the most highly prized spice on the East–West trade routes. The pepper vine *Piper nigrum* is native to the tropical coast of west India but is now grown throughout the equatorial regions of the world. The vine sends out spiky stems burdened with small yellow-green flowers and, most importantly, peppercorns—50 or 60 per stem, like a bunch of immature grapes.

rock salt

Rock salt is mined from underground and then evaporated, to be crystallised to the desired degree of fineness. Rock salt is only used in its crude form for preservation purposes and for use in ice cream machines and so on. In its refined form it is sold for use in the kitchen. The flavour will depend on any impurities left in the salt.

flaked sea salt

Sea salt is produced by the evaporation of sea water from salt marshes. More costly to produce than other salts, sea salt flakes are odourless but have a strong taste. The best sea salt is made by drawing sea water into large shallow 'basins' and leaving it to evaporate in the heat of the sun. The top pure-white layer of salt fetches the highest price and has the most superior taste. When using flaked sea salt, crush it between your fingers before adding to food.

green and white peppercorns

Green peppercorns are the immature peppercorns of the pepper vine. They are available fresh, freeze-dried or pickled in a brine solution. Fresh peppercorns have a pungent and zesty flavour and are best used in cooking. Green peppercorns are softer in texture and milder in flavour than black or white peppercorns.

White pepper is less aromatic than black pepper but has a sharper flavour. It is often used when the flavour of pepper is required but the black pepper specks are not.

black peppercorns

These are simply green peppercorns that have been allowed to ripen on the vine and then sun-dried until they harden and shrivel. Black pepper, the strongest-tasting pepper of all, has a hint of sweetness. All pepper loses its flavour a few months after being ground, so always grind it fresh from a pepper mill. The finer the grind, the less bite the pepper will have, because the peppercorn's flavour-giving oils are more dispersed.

szechwan pepper

Szechwan pepper is also not a true pepper. Obtained from the berries of the prickly ash, a tree native to the Szechwan province of China, the reddish-brown berries are dried after picking and are husked to remove the small, bitter, black seeds, which are then crushed. Szechwan pepper has a spicy, earthy flavour and produces a slight numbing effect when eaten. Maximise flavour by dry-roasting the peppercorns before grinding.

pink peppercorns

Not really pepper at all, pink peppercorns are the fruit of a South American shrub which was transplanted to the island of Réunion, east of Madagascar—an exotic pedigree for a spice that, although decorative, has very little bite.

flaked sea salt

rock salt

black peppercorns

szechwan pepper   white and green peppercorns

pink peppercorns

good ideas

too salty

Ever purchased olives that
taste more of salt than of
fruity olives? If so, soak
them in cold water for
an hour or so to remove
some of the salt flavour.

pepper pasta

This simple side dish of hot pasta
tossed with butter, freshly cracked
black pepper and sea salt can be
served with almost anything.

the cure

Make a simple gravlax* by packing a salmon fillet
in rock salt, a little sugar and some dill sprigs.
Cover and refrigerate overnight. Scrape away the
salt, sugar and dill and serve in thin slices on
toasted bagels with crème fraîche* or sour cream.

salt roast

Place some small new potatoes, a dash of olive oil, some rosemary sprigs and a good pinch of flaked sea salt in a baking dish. Roast in a hot oven until soft and golden.

flavoured salts

These are easy to make and will enhance the flavour of many foods. Grind together flaked sea salt and lemon rind and use on fish or chicken, or try mixing chopped red chillies with salt to use on potatoes or meats. Toasted cumin seeds mixed with salt makes the perfect accompaniment to lamb.

peppered ricotta

Fill a loaf tin with fresh ricotta that has been mixed with cracked pepper. Bake at 180°C (350°F) for 45 minutes or until firm. Turn onto a baking tray, splash with olive oil and extra pepper and bake again until golden. Serve on bread or as part of a salad.

pepper steak

Pepper steak is best the way the French make it. Press freshly ground black pepper into steaks and cook in a hot frying pan until cooked to your liking.

chicken with rocket sauce

pepper-crusted tuna with asian salad

salt-baked fish

chicken with rocket sauce

4 chicken breast fillets
olive oil, for brushing
cracked black pepper
150g (5 oz) snow pea shoots
rocket sauce
1½ cups shredded rocket (arugula)
¼ cup chopped fresh dill
¼ cup chopped fresh flat-leaf parsley
2 cloves garlic, sliced
1 tablespoon Dijon mustard
2 tablespoons salted capers*, rinsed
½ cup olive oil
2 tablespoons lemon juice

To make the rocket sauce, place the rocket, dill, parsley, garlic, mustard and capers into a food processor and process until smooth. Add the oil and lemon juice and process until combined.
Brush the chicken breasts with a little oil and sprinkle with cracked black pepper. Place the chicken in a steamer over rapidly simmering water and steam for 3–5 minutes or until just cooked through.
To serve, slice each chicken breast into 3 pieces. Pile snow pea shoots onto serving plates and top with the chicken. Spoon over the rocket sauce and serve. Serves 4.

pepper-crusted tuna with asian salad

2 tablespoons green peppercorns in brine, drained
1 tablespoon peanut oil
500g (1 lb) sashimi* tuna
Asian salad
100g (3½ oz) Asian salad leaves
1 Lebanese cucumber, shredded
5 kaffir lime leaves, shredded
2 tablespoons soy sauce
1 tablespoon brown sugar
1 tablespoon lime juice
¾ cup fresh coriander (cilantro) leaves

Lightly crush the peppercorns in a mortar and pestle and place them on a flat plate. Brush the oil over the tuna and then press the tuna into the peppercorns. Heat a frying pan, grill pan or barbecue over medium–high heat. Cook the tuna for 1–2 minutes each side, or until well seared and cooked to your liking.
To make the Asian salad, place the salad leaves, cucumber, lime leaves, soy sauce, sugar, lime juice and coriander leaves in a bowl and toss well to combine.
To serve, place the salad on serving plates. Slice the tuna and place on top of the salad. The tuna can be served warm or cold. Serves 4.

salt-baked fish

4 x 350–400g (11–13 oz) small whole fish such as snapper, gutted
cracked black pepper
12 sprigs fresh flat-leaf parsley
4–5kg (8–10 lb) coarse rock salt

Preheat the oven to 220°C (425°F). Wash the fish and pat dry. Sprinkle the inside cavities of the fish well with pepper and stuff with the parsley sprigs.
Spread two baking trays with half the salt. Place the fish on the baking trays and then cover with the remaining salt. Press the salt firmly around the fish and sprinkle with a little water. Bake for 15 minutes, then allow the fish to rest on the trays for 5 minutes.
To serve, remove the salt in large pieces and place the fish on serving plates. Serve with a green salad and lemon wedges. Serves 4.

szechwan fried pork with rice noodle rolls

2 tablespoons Szechwan peppercorns
1 teaspoon flaked sea salt
600g (1¼ lb) pork fillet, trimmed
1 tablespoon peanut oil
500g (1 lb) packet rice noodle rolls*
4 bok choy*, halved
2 tablespoons shredded ginger
kecap manis*, to serve

Place the peppercorns in a dry frying pan over medium heat and toast until fragrant. Place in a mortar and pestle with the salt and crush lightly together. Sprinkle the pork well with the pepper and salt mixture.
Heat the oil in a frying pan over medium–high heat. Add the pork fillet and cook for 3 minutes each side, or until cooked to your liking. Allow the pork to stand in the pan for 3 minutes.
While the pork is cooking, place the rice noodle rolls and bok choy into a steamer and sprinkle with ginger. Place the steamer over boiling water and cook for 3–5 minutes or until the noodles are soft.
To serve, place the greens and noodle rolls on serving plates and drizzle with kecap manis. Slice the pork and place on top. Serves 4.

szechwan fried pork with rice noodle rolls

sweet potato cakes with peppered beef

olive and lemon simmered lamb

sweet potato cakes with peppered beef

750g (1 1/2 lb) orange sweet potato (kumera), peeled and grated
2 eggs
2 tablespoons plain (all-purpose) flour
1/2 cup grated parmesan cheese
cracked black pepper
oil, for frying
400g (13 oz) eye fillet steaks
cracked black pepper, extra
100g (3 1/2 oz) baby rocket (arugula) leaves
150g (5 oz) soft goats' cheese

To make the sweet potato cakes, combine the grated sweet potato, eggs, flour, parmesan and pepper. Heat 5mm (1/4 inch) of oil in a frying pan over medium–high heat. Add a few spoonfuls of the mixture to the pan and flatten with a spatula. Cook for 2 minutes each side or until the cakes are golden and crisp. Place on absorbent paper and keep warm in the oven.

To make the peppered beef, press the eye fillet steaks into the extra cracked pepper and cook in a hot non-stick frying pan over medium–high heat. Cook for 3–4 minutes on each side or until cooked to your liking. Leave the beef for 3 minutes before thinly slicing.

To serve, place 3 sweet potato cakes on each serving plate and top with the rocket, goats' cheese and sliced beef. Drizzle with olive oil and lemon juice to serve. Serves 4.

olive and lemon simmered lamb

8 lean lamb leg chops, trimmed
rice flour, for coating
1 tablespoon olive oil
4 cloves garlic, halved
3/4 cup (6 fl oz) dry white wine
3 1/4 cups (26 fl oz) chicken or beef stock
8 sprigs fresh thyme
1 tablespoon shredded lemon rind
200g (6 1/2 oz) green olives, pitted
cracked black pepper

Lightly dust the lamb chops with rice flour and shake well to remove any excess. Heat the oil in a large, deep frying pan over medium heat. Add the chops and cook for 3 minutes each side or until sealed.

Add the garlic, wine, stock, thyme and lemon rind and reduce the heat. Cover and simmer for 1 hour, turning the lamb once.

Stir through the olives and cracked black pepper and cook uncovered for a further 25 minutes or until the lamb is tender and the sauce has thickened. Serve the lamb with its pan sauce, creamy mashed potatoes and steamed green beans. Serves 4.

note – Check the olives for saltiness before adding them to the sauce. If they are too salty for your liking, soak in cold water for a few hours beforehand.

beef and peppercorn pies

1 quantity shortcrust pastry* or 375g (12 oz)
   ready-prepared pastry
300g (10 oz) ready-prepared puff pastry
1 egg, lightly beaten
filling
2 teaspoons olive oil
1 onion, finely chopped
1 tablespoon green peppercorns in brine, drained
800g (1 lb 10 oz) blade steak, cubed
1 cup (8 fl oz) beef stock
1/3 cup (2¾ fl oz) red wine
1 tablespoon cornflour (cornstarch)
2 tablespoons water

To make the filling, heat the oil in a saucepan over medium heat. Add the onion and cook for 3 minutes. Lightly crush the peppercorns and add to the pan with the steak. Cook for 5 minutes or until the meat is sealed. Add the stock and wine to the pan; cover and simmer for 45 minutes or until the beef is tender. Mix the cornflour and water to make a smooth paste and add to the saucepan. Cook, stirring for 2 minutes, then remove from the heat and leave to cool. Preheat the oven to 200°C (400°F). Roll out the shortcrust pastry on a lightly floured surface. Cut the pastry to fit four deep 8cm (3 inch) individual pie tins. Roll out the puff pastry on a lightly floured surface and cut circles for the lids. Fill the shortcrust pastry with the beef filling and then top with a puff pastry lid, pressing gently to seal. Brush the pastry tops with egg and bake for 15 minutes or until the pastry is golden and puffed. Serve warm. Makes 4.

fish with crispy caper dressing

4 x 180g (6 oz) pieces firm white fish, such as blue eye cod
2 tablespoons olive oil
sea salt and cracked black pepper
1 tablespoon fresh lemon thyme leaves
4 baby cos lettuces, halved
crispy caper dressing
2 tablespoons salted capers*, drained
2 tablespoons butter
2 tablespoons olive oil
2 tablespoons lemon juice

Brush the fish with the olive oil. Sprinkle both sides with salt, pepper and thyme. Cook the fish on a hot grill or barbecue for 2 minutes each side, or until cooked to your liking. Set aside.
To make the dressing, place the capers, butter and olive oil in a frying pan over medium heat and cook for 4 minutes or until the capers are crisp. Remove from the heat and add lemon juice. To serve, place the lettuce halves and fish on serving plates and pour over the caper dressing. Serves 4.

salted szechwan pepper prawns

1kg (2 lb) medium green (raw) prawns
1½ tablespoons Szechwan peppercorns
1 tablespoon flaked sea salt
3 tablespoons rice flour
peanut oil, for shallow-frying
stir-fried bean sprouts
2 teaspoons sesame oil*
2 red chillies, seeded and chopped
200g (6½ oz) bean sprouts
400g (13 oz) Chinese cabbage, shredded
2 tablespoons lime juice
2 tablespoons soy sauce
1/3 cup chopped fresh coriander (cilantro) leaves

Peel and clean the prawns, leaving the tails intact. Place the Szechwan peppercorns in a dry frying pan and toast over medium heat for 1–2 minutes. Place the toasted peppercorns, salt and rice flour in a mortar and pestle and grind into a coarse powder.
Toss the prawns in the pepper mixture. Heat the oil in a frying pan over medium–high heat. Add the prawns a few at a time and cook for 1 minute each side. Place the prawns on absorbent paper and keep warm.
To stir-fry the bean sprouts, heat the sesame oil in a frying pan over high heat. Add the chillies and cook for 1 minute. Add the bean sprouts, cabbage, lime juice and soy sauce and stir-fry for 1 minute. Stir through the coriander and pile onto serving plates. Top with the prawns and serve. Serves 4.

salt and pepper chicken

150g (5 oz) dry rice-stick noodles*
2 teaspoons sesame oil*
4 spring (green) onions, chopped
3 tablespoons lemon juice
1/4 cup fresh coriander (cilantro) leaves
4 chicken breast fillets
1½ teaspoons Chinese five-spice powder
2 teaspoons flaked sea salt
1 teaspoon cracked black pepper
1 tablespoon peanut oil

Place the noodles in a saucepan of boiling water and cook for 2 minutes or until soft. Drain. Heat the sesame oil in a frying pan over medium–high heat. Add the spring onions and cook for 1 minute. Add the noodles, lemon juice and coriander to the pan and toss to combine.
Cut each chicken fillet into 4 pieces. Combine the five-spice, salt and pepper in a bowl and mix well. Sprinkle over both sides of the chicken. Heat the peanut oil in a frying pan over high heat. Add the chicken pieces a few at a time and cook for 2 minutes each side or until cooked. To serve, place the noodles in bowls and top with chicken. Serves 4.

beef and peppercorn pies

salted szechwan pepper prawns

fish with crispy caper dressing

salt and pepper chicken

basil+mint

basics

No two herbs enjoy such widespread use as aromatic basil and sweetly-scented mint.

Basil is native to India but can be found throughout South-East Asia, North-East Africa and the Mediterranean. This annual herb was introduced to Europe in the 16th century and to this day still has a strong association with Italian cooking. There are more than 40 varieties of basil, the best-known being sweet, bush, red and Thai basil.

Mint originated in Greece and travelled to many other European nations (including England, where it achieved fame as a sauce), as well as to the Middle East. The Asians also enjoyed the fresh, cleansing taste of this herb. There are as many as 30 varieties of mint, the most popular being spearmint, wintermint (otherwise known as common or garden mint) and Vietnamese mint.

mint

Common or garden mint, with rounded leaves and a fresh, sweet smell, is most often found growing in gardens or pots and can be used in both sweet and savoury recipes. Remove the leaves from the stem before chopping or using whole.

basil

The leaves of this herb are shiny and bright green and have a strong, sweet aniseed aroma. If you are growing your own basil, pick out the flower heads to extend the plant's leaf-producing life. When buying basil, look for bunches without any blackened or limp leaves. Use only the leaves of the plant, and tear or cut them as desired. Note that basil will darken if it is bruised, and also when it is added to anything hot.

thai basil

Also known as Asian or holy basil (the 'holy' description deriving from the fact that it is often planted around temples), this strongly flavoured variety of basil is used extensively in Thai cooking. The leaves are smaller than those of sweet basil and have a purple-reddish tint to the young leaves and stems. Thai basil has a strong aniseed flavour and is best used in well-flavoured dishes such as curries or spicy stir-fries.

spearmint

A native of the Mediterranean, spearmint is the most common mint available commercially. The long, narrow leaves have serrated edges and a fresh, distinctive flavour. This mint can be used in both sweet and savoury recipes. Remove the leaves from the stem and chop.

vietnamese mint

This piquant herb, also known as laksa leaf, Cambodian mint or hot mint, is not actually a true mint. The narrow, pointed, purple-tinged leaves have a hot, peppery, acidic taste. Vietnamese mint is an essential ingredient in the Singaporean/Malaysian soup laksa and is also commonly used in Thai salads, Vietnamese spring rolls and salads.

spearmint

sweet basil

common mint

thai basil

vietnamese mint

good ideas

infused oil

Blanch 1 cup of fresh mint or basil leaves in boiling water then dry well. Place the herbs in a food processor with 1 cup (8 fl oz) of olive oil and process until smooth. Strain through muslin and refrigerate for up to 3 weeks. Use as a base for frying fish or chicken, or in salad dressings.

basil-roasted tomatoes

Place halved tomatoes on a baking tray, cut-side up, and sprinkle with basil leaves, olive oil and pepper. Roast in a preheated 200°C (400°F) oven for 35 minutes or until soft.

pesto

Place 1 cup of basil leaves, or a combination of basil, mint or coriander, in a food processor with 3 tablespoons of both pine nuts and grated parmesan cheese and a crushed clove of garlic. Add enough olive oil to form a smooth paste.

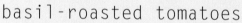

basil and parmesan wafers

Combine 2 tablespoons of grated parmesan cheese with 2 teaspoons of shredded basil. Place on a baking tray lined with non-stick baking paper and spread the mixture to form a flat disk. Bake in a preheated 200°C (400°F) oven for 5 minutes. Cool on the tray.

basil feta

Place feta cheese in a bowl and cover with extra-virgin olive oil, lots of basil leaves and some peppercorns. Refrigerate for 4 hours before serving with slices of crusty wood-fired bread.

minted syrup

Make a sugar syrup using 1½ cups (12 fl oz) of water and 1 cup of sugar. Add 1 cup of shredded mint and simmer for 3 minutes. Strain and serve the syrup with soda water, gin and lemon, or in champagne.

mint refresher

Place 2 teaspoons of green tea, 14 mint leaves and 1 tablespoon of sugar in a saucepan with 2½ cups (20 fl oz) of water and simmer for 3 minutes. Strain into glasses and serve warm.

crisp salmon with minted broad bean salad

basil-fried tomato and couscous salad

beetroot and mint salad

crisp salmon with minted broad bean salad

4 x 180g (6 oz) pieces salmon fillet, skin on
sea salt and cracked black pepper
2 tablespoons olive oil
minted broad bean salad
650g (1 lb 5 oz) shelled broad beans
3/4 cup shredded fresh mint
3 tablespoons lemon juice
2 tablespoons extra-virgin olive oil
1 tablespoon wholegrain mustard

To make the salad, place the broad beans in a saucepan
of boiling water and cook for 5 minutes or until tender.
Drain and cool under running water. Remove the skins
from the beans and combine them with the mint, lemon
juice, olive oil and mustard.
Sprinkle the skin of the salmon with sea salt and black
pepper. Heat the oil in a frying pan over high heat and
add the salmon, skin-side down. Cook for 4 minutes or
until the skin is golden and crisp. Turn and cook the other
side for 1 minute.
To serve, pile the broad beans onto serving plates and top
with the salmon. Serve with lemon wedges. Serves 4.

basil-fried tomato and couscous salad

1 cup couscous*
1 1/2 cups (12 fl oz) chicken or vegetable stock, boiling
sea salt and cracked black pepper
150g (5 oz) baby English spinach leaves
1/2 cup grated parmesan cheese
balsamic vinegar, to serve
basil-fried tomatoes
2 tablespoons olive oil
3 ripe tomatoes, thickly sliced
1/2 cup shredded fresh basil

Place the couscous in a bowl, pour over the boiling
chicken or vegetable stock, and stir in some salt and
pepper. Cover with plastic wrap and allow to stand for
5 minutes or until the liquid has been absorbed.
To cook the tomatoes, heat the oil in a frying pan over
medium heat. Press both sides of the tomatoes into the
basil and place in the hot pan. Cook for 3 minutes each
side or until the tomatoes are golden.
To serve, place the spinach leaves on serving plates and
top with the couscous. Sprinkle with parmesan and
balsamic vinegar then top with the basil-fried tomatoes.
Serves 4.

beetroot and mint salad

6 beetroots, peeled
1/4 cup (2 fl oz) balsamic vinegar
cracked black pepper
2 tablespoons wholegrain mustard
mint salad
1 cup shredded fresh mint
150g (5 oz) salad leaves
200g (6 1/2 oz) marinated feta in oil, crumbled
1 tablespoon olive oil

Place the beetroots in a saucepan of boiling water and
cook for 25–35 minutes or until soft. Drain and cut the
beetroots into wedges. Toss with balsamic vinegar, pepper
and mustard and set aside to cool.
To make the mint salad, place the mint, salad leaves,
feta and olive oil in a bowl and toss to combine. To serve,
place the mint salad on serving plates and top with the
beetroot. Serve with grilled bread slices. Serves 4.

veal cutlets with minted pea purée

4 veal cutlets
cracked black pepper
2 tablespoons olive oil
3 tablespoons fresh mint leaves
minted pea purée
3 waxy potatoes, whole and unpeeled
60g (2 oz) butter
3/4 cup (6 fl oz) cream
sea salt
2 cups fresh peas
2 tablespoons chopped fresh mint

To make the minted pea purée, place the potatoes in a
saucepan of boiling water and cook over medium–high
heat for 12–15 minutes or until soft. Drain and cool slightly,
then press to remove the skins. Return the potatoes to
the saucepan and mash well. Return the saucepan to the
warm stovetop, add the butter, cream and salt and whip
with a whisk until smooth. Keep the mash warm.
Place the peas in a saucepan of boiling water and cook
for 5 minutes or until tender. Drain. Place the peas, mint
and a few spoonfuls of the mash in a food processor and
process until smooth. Add the peas to the potato and stir
over low heat to warm.
To cook the veal, sprinkle the meat well with pepper.
Heat the oil in a frying pan over medium–high heat, add
the veal and mint and cook for 4–5 minutes each side or
until the veal is cooked to your liking and the mint is crisp.
To serve, place the minted pea purée on serving plates
and top with veal cutlets and the crisp mint. Serves 4.

veal cutlets with minted pea purée

chicken in basil and coconut broth

3 cups (24 fl oz) coconut cream
3 cups (24 fl oz) chicken stock
2 tablespoons shredded ginger
2 red chillies, seeded and chopped
1 tablespoon fish sauce*
3 fresh coriander (cilantro) roots, bruised
3 chicken breast fillets, sliced
1 cup shredded fresh basil
100g (3½ oz) bean sprouts

Place the coconut cream, chicken stock, ginger, chillies, fish sauce and coriander roots in a large, deep frying pan over medium heat and bring to a slow boil. Allow the broth to simmer for 5 minutes.
Add the chicken to the pan and stir. Cook for 5 minutes or until the chicken is cooked through. Stir through the shredded basil. Pile the bean sprouts into shallow serving bowls, top with the chicken and spoon the broth over the top. Serves 4.

tomato, basil and ricotta tart

4 tomatoes, halved
2 tablespoons olive oil
cracked black pepper
375g (12 oz) ready-prepared puff pastry
185g (6 oz) fresh ricotta cheese
¾ cup grated parmesan cheese
2 eggs
¾ cup shredded fresh basil

Preheat the oven to 180°C (350°F). Place the tomatoes on a baking tray and sprinkle with olive oil and pepper. Bake for 50 minutes or until soft and slightly dried.
Roll out the puff pastry on a lightly floured surface until 3mm (⅛ inch) thick. Cut the pastry into a 20 x 30cm (8 x 12 inch) rectangle and place on a baking tray lined with non-stick baking paper.
Place the ricotta in a fine sieve and press to remove any excess liquid. Place the ricotta, parmesan and eggs in a food processor and process until smooth, then stir through the basil. Spread the ricotta filling over the pastry base, leaving a 2cm (¾ inch) border, then press the tomatoes into the ricotta filling.
Bake for 30 minutes or until the filling is set and the pastry is golden. Serve in slices with a salad or with sliced grilled meats. Serves 4–6.

chicken in basil and coconut broth

tomato, basil and ricotta tart

pasta with fresh tomatoes and mint

450g (14 oz) spaghetti
4 ripe tomatoes, finely chopped
1 cup shredded fresh mint
1/2 cup shredded fresh parsley
2 tablespoons salted capers*, rinsed
2 tablespoons lemon juice
1 tablespoon fruity olive oil
sea salt and cracked black pepper
1/2 cup finely grated parmesan cheese

Cook the spaghetti in a large saucepan of rapidly boiling water until al dente. Drain.
Mix together the tomatoes, mint, parsley, capers, lemon juice, olive oil, salt and pepper.
Pile the spaghetti into bowls and top with the tomato and mint sauce. Sprinkle with parmesan and serve with slices of crusty wood-fired bread. Serves 4.
note – It is best to use very ripe tomatoes for this recipe.

lemongrass, prawn and mint soup

600g (1 1/4 lb) green (raw) prawns
6 cups (48 fl oz) water
3 tablespoons soy sauce
3 stalks lemongrass*, bruised
2 slices ginger
1–2 red chillies, sliced
4 kaffir lime leaves, shredded
100g (3 1/2 oz) rice vermicelli noodles*
1/4 cup shredded fresh Vietnamese mint

Peel the prawns and place the tails, shells and heads in a deep non-stick frying pan over medium heat until the shells are well coloured. Add the water to the pan, bring to the boil and allow to simmer for 2 minutes, skimming the surface occasionally to keep the prawn stock clear. Drain through a fine sieve and discard the prawn pieces.
Place the prawn stock, soy sauce, lemongrass, ginger, chilli and kaffir lime leaves in a saucepan and simmer over low heat for 5 minutes.
Place the noodles in a bowl and cover with boiling water. Leave for 5 minutes, then drain.
Add the prawns to the broth in the saucepan and cook for 2 minutes or until the prawns are tender.
Divide the noodles among serving bowls. Stir the Vietnamese mint through the soup, then ladle over the noodles. Serve with lime and extra chilli. Serves 4.

pork and vietnamese mint noodles

250g (8 oz) dry rice vermicelli noodles*
1 cup small fresh Thai basil leaves
1/2 cup shredded fresh Vietnamese mint
1/3 cup (2 3/4 fl oz) lime juice
2 tablespoons fish sauce*
2 tablespoons sugar
600g (1 1/4 lb) pork fillet, trimmed
1 tablespoon peanut oil
2 teaspoons sesame oil*
sesame seeds

Cook the rice noodles in a saucepan of boiling water for 2–3 minutes or until soft. Drain, rinse under cold water and drain again.
Toss the noodles with the basil and mint. Combine the lime juice, fish sauce and sugar, add to the noodles and toss well. Brush the pork with the combined peanut oil and sesame oil and coat with sesame seeds. Cook the pork in a hot frying pan for 3 minutes each side or until cooked through.
To serve, place the noodles on serving plates and top with the sliced pork. Serves 4.

basil and tomato bread soup

12 very ripe tomatoes
2 tablespoons olive oil
2 cloves garlic, crushed
3 cups (24 fl oz) vegetable stock
250g (8 oz) wood-fired bread
1 cup fresh basil leaves, torn in half
sea salt and cracked black pepper
grated parmesan cheese, to serve

Score a cross in the skin on the base of each tomato. Place the tomatoes in a large saucepan of boiling water for 5 minutes. Drain. Peel away the tomato skins and cut the tomatoes into quarters.
Heat the oil in a large saucepan over medium heat. Add the garlic and cook for 1 minute. Add the tomatoes and vegetable stock to the pan and simmer, uncovered, for 30 minutes or until the tomatoes are very soft.
Remove the crusts from the bread and chop the loaf into rough cubes. Add the bread, basil leaves and lots of salt and pepper to the saucepan and stir for 3 minutes or until heated through.
Serve the soup in bowls with a sprinkling of pepper and parmesan cheese. Serves 4.

pasta with fresh tomatoes and mint

pork and vietnamese mint noodles

lemongrass, prawn and mint soup

basil and tomato bread soup

melon and papaya in mint and ginger syrup

grilled ruby grapefruit   pistachio baklava with mint syrup

melon and papaya in mint and ginger syrup

½ honeydew melon
½ papaya
shredded fresh mint, to serve
mint and ginger syrup
1 cup (8 fl oz) water
½ cup sugar
1 tablespoon shredded ginger
¼ cup shredded fresh mint
1 tablespoon lime juice

To make the mint and ginger syrup, place the water, sugar, ginger, mint and lime juice in a saucepan over medium heat and stir to dissolve the sugar. Allow to simmer for 10 minutes, then cool the syrup.
Peel the honeydew melon and papaya and cut into small, thick wedges. To serve, place the melon and papaya on serving plates and spoon over the syrup. Sprinkle with shredded mint and serve as a dessert, or for breakfast with thick yoghurt. Serves 4.

grilled ruby grapefruit

2 ruby grapefruits
½ cup sugar
⅓ cup chopped fresh mint

Halve the grapefruits. Place the sugar and mint in a food processor and process until finely chopped. Press the grapefruit into the sugar and mint mixture and place, cut-side down, in a hot frying pan and cook for 4 minutes or until golden, caramelised and warm.
Serve for breakfast, brunch or dessert. Serves 4.

pistachio baklava with mint syrup

36 sheets filo (phyllo) pastry, 20 x 30cm (8 x 12 inches)
85g (3 oz) butter, melted
2 tablespoons vegetable oil
filling
1½ cups chopped walnuts
1½ cups chopped unsalted pistachio nuts
1 teaspoon ground cinnamon
⅓ cup brown sugar
45g (1½ oz) butter
mint syrup
¾ cup (6 fl oz) water
1½ cups sugar
½ cup shredded fresh mint leaves
1 teaspoon rosewater*

Preheat the oven to 160°C (315°F).
To make the filling, place the walnuts, pistachios, cinnamon, sugar and butter in a food processor and process until finely chopped. Place a sheet of filo pastry in a 20 x 30cm (8 x 12 inch) cake tin and brush with the combined melted butter and oil. Top with 11 more sheets of filo, brushing each sheet well with the butter and oil mixture. Spread half the filling over the top. Top with 12 more filo sheets, brushing with the butter and oil mixture as you go. Sprinkle evenly with the remaining filling and then top with the remaining pastry sheets, brushing as you go with the remaining butter and oil. Cut the baklava into diamond shapes in the tin. Bake for 1 hour.
To make the mint syrup, place the water, sugar and mint in a small saucepan over low heat and stir until the sugar has dissolved. Simmer for 6 minutes, then strain to remove the mint leaves. Add the rosewater.
When the baklava is cooked, let stand for 5 minutes, then pour the syrup over the top. Serve warm or cold with strong coffee. Serves 12.

whipped minted yoghurt

¼ cup sugar
½ cup shredded fresh mint leaves
½ cup (4 fl oz) water
1 cup (8 fl oz) yoghurt, well chilled
1 cup (8 fl oz) cream, well chilled

Place the sugar, mint and water in a saucepan over low heat and stir until the sugar has dissolved. Simmer for 4 minutes, then stand for 5 minutes. Strain and cool.
Place the yoghurt, cream and mint syrup in the bowl of an electric mixer and beat until light and creamy.
Serve the minted yoghurt with fresh fruits for breakfast or dessert. Garnish with extra mint leaves. Serves 4.

whipped minted yoghurt

cinnamon +spice

basics

Spices have played an important part not only in the history of food but also in trading. The opening up of trade routes between East and West was due in large part to the demand for spices in Europe. Spices served a dual purpose: they enlivened an otherwise fairly bland diet, and they disguised the scent and flavour of none-too-fresh foodstuffs.

From the earliest times, one of the most eagerly sought-after spices was cinnamon, the aromatic bark of the tropical Asian laurel tree. Treacherous journeys, complicated political manoeuvres and territorial invasion were all undertaken to procure this precious spice, which in the 16th and 17th centuries rivalled gold in value. Along with its sister spices from Asia, amongst them coriander, cloves, fennel and star anise, cinnamon remains to this day one of the most popular cooking flavourings in dishes both sweet and savoury.

star anise

A staple in Chinese and Vietnamese cooking, this beautiful spice is the sun-dried fruit of a member of the magnolia family native to those countries. The fruit, an eight-pointed star in which the carpels provide most of the flavour and aroma, imparts a delicate fragrance and a pronounced sweet liquorice flavour. Star anise is usually sold whole or sometimes as broken pieces.

coriander and cumin seeds

Coriander or cilantro, the green leafy herb used extensively in South-East Asian cooking, is related to the parsley family. The seeds that come from this fragrant herb are dried and used as an aromatic spice in many dishes, the most popular being curries. Coriander seeds should be toasted and often ground before being used.

Cumin is also a member of the parsley family and is native to the Mediterranean region. The golden-brown seeds can be purchased ground, although the flavour is stronger if the seeds are bought whole then ground in a mortar and pestle when needed. Dry-roasting the seeds before grinding releases the flavour further. Cumin seeds have a distinctively strong aroma and a lingering, bittersweet, earthy flavour.

cinnamon sticks

Cinnamon is the soft inner bark of the cinnamon tree, a camphor laurel indigenous to Sri Lanka. As the bark dries and contracts, it rolls itself into tight quills that have a sweet aroma and a warm, intense flavour. Powdered or ground cinnamon tends to stale quickly. Cinnamon sticks, on the other hand, retain their flavour for a longer time, and the quills are easy to grind in a spice grinder. Whole cinnamon sticks should be removed from a dish and discarded after cooking.

juniper berries

A cypress native to the British Isles and commonly grown in northern Europe, the evergreen juniper tree produces small purplish-blue berries that have a resinous flavour. Juniper berries are used in northern European cuisines in marinades and pâtés, and with pork, game and poultry. But perhaps juniper berries are best known for the flavour and aroma they impart to gin. To release their flavour, lightly crush the berries in a mortar and pestle or grind them in a pepper mill.

chinese five-spice

This blend of ground spices is one of the most versatile around. Its proclaimed purpose is to touch all the senses of the palate: salty, sweet, sour, pungent and bitter. Five-spice is a well-balanced mix of Szechwan pepper, cinnamon or cassia, clove, fennel seeds and star anise. The ratio of ingredients varies from region to region and maker to maker.

chinese five-spice

cinnamon sticks

star anise

cumin and coriander seeds

juniper berries

163

good ideas

chinese stock

Add an Asian flavour to your basic chicken stock by adding a star anise and a cinnamon stick. For more spice, add a halved chilli, a few slices of ginger and a splash of Chinese rice wine.

mulled wine

Heat red wine together with pieces of orange rind, cinnamon sticks and a few cloves. Pour into mugs and drink warm on a cold winter's night.

cinnamon sugar

Grind cinnamon sticks in a spice grinder to make a powder, then stir through sugar. Sprinkle over French toast or pancakes, or use to flavour custards or ice cream.

maximum flavour

Spices have a better flavour if you grind them fresh. Use a mortar and pestle or a spice grinder.

easy move

When adding whole spices that need to be removed from the dish at the end of the cooking time, wrap them together in muslin. Alternatively, larger spices like cinnamon sticks can be wrapped in bay leaves held with string.

stuff it

Juniper berries make a great addition to a stuffing for game birds, turkey and pork. Simply toss lightly crushed juniper berries through your fresh breadcrumb stuffing.

hot toddy

Splash a good dash of rum into a tumbler, add a few cloves and a cinnamon stick and top up with hot water. Sweeten with a little sugar or honey. This drink should cure anything from the chills to the blues.

laksa with coriander-crusted chicken

chilli and spice squid

chicken simmered with juniper berries

laska with coriander-crusted chicken

200g (6½ oz) dried rice vermicelli noodles*
2–4 tablespoons laksa paste* (see note below)
2 cups (16 fl oz) coconut milk
4 cups (32 fl oz) chicken stock
3 fresh coriander (cilantro) roots, bruised
4 kaffir lime leaves, shredded
4 small bok choy*, quartered
150g (5 oz) bean sprouts
coriander-crusted chicken
3 chicken breast fillets
2 tablespoons peanut oil
½ cup finely chopped fresh coriander (cilantro) leaves

Place the rice noodles in a bowl and cover with boiling water. Allow to stand for 5 minutes, then drain.
Place the laksa paste in a saucepan over medium heat and stir for 1 minute or until fragrant. Add the coconut milk, chicken stock, coriander roots and kaffir lime leaves and simmer for 5 minutes. Add the bok choy and cook for a further 4 minutes.
To make the coriander-crusted chicken, cut the chicken breasts into thick, flat pieces. Heat the oil in a frying pan over medium heat. Add the coriander to the pan, then add the chicken and cook for 1 minute each side or until tender. To serve, place bean sprouts and noodles in each serving bowl, then ladle the soup into the bowls and top with the chicken. Serves 4.
note – You may need to check the heat of the chillies in the laksa paste by tasting a little bit before cooking. Chilli heat can by reduced by adding a little sugar. Increase the heat by adding a few chopped seeded chillies.

chicken simmered with juniper berries

2 cups (16 fl oz) chicken stock
1 tablespoon juniper berries, lightly crushed
½ cup (4 fl oz) verjuice*
3 sprigs fresh thyme
4 chicken breast fillets

Place the chicken stock, juniper berries, verjuice and thyme in a deep frying pan over low heat and allow to simmer for 3 minutes. Add the chicken fillets to the pan and simmer for 6–7 minutes each side or until tender.
Remove the chicken from the pan and keep warm. Increase the temperature to high and boil the pan liquid for 2 minutes or until it has thickened slightly. To serve, place the chicken on serving plates and top with the pan sauce. Serve with creamy mashed potato. Serves 4.

chilli and spice squid

12 small squid, cleaned and quartered
2 egg whites, lightly beaten
peanut oil, for deep-frying
chilli–salt mixture
3 red chillies, seeded and chopped
2 tablespoons flaked sea salt
2 teaspoons cracked black pepper
3 teaspoons Chinese five-spice powder
1 cup rice flour

To make the chilli–salt mixture, place the chillies, salt, pepper and Chinese five-spice in a spice grinder or mortar and pestle and grind together. Add the rice flour and mix well to combine.
Wash the squid and pat dry. Score one side of the squid with the tip of a knife. Lightly dip the squid into the egg white and then press into the chilli–salt mixture to coat. Heat the oil in a deep saucepan over medium–high heat. Add the squid a few pieces at a time and cook for 30 seconds or until lightly golden. Drain on absorbent paper and serve with chilli sauce, Asian salad greens and a wedge of lime. Serves 4.

juniper roast pork and figs

750g (1½ lb) boneless pork loin
2 tablespoons olive oil
2 tablespoons juniper berries, lightly crushed
1 bunch fresh oregano
cracked black pepper
4 large fresh figs, halved
extra olive oil, for drizzling

Preheat the oven to 220°C (425°F). Trim the pork loin of any fat or sinew. Heat the oil in a frying pan over medium–high heat. Add the juniper berries and cook for 30 seconds. Add the pork loin and cook for 2 minutes each side, or until well browned.
Place the oregano in a pile on a baking tray, then top with the pork. Sprinkle the pork with the juniper berries and the oil from the pan, and top with cracked black pepper. Bake the pork for 5 minutes, then add the figs to the pan and drizzle with the extra oil. Cook for a further 10 minutes or until the pork is cooked to your liking.
To serve, slice the pork into pieces and place on a serving plate with the figs. Spoon over the pan juices and serve with creamy mashed potato. Serves 4.

juniper roast pork and figs

roast spice lamb and eggplant

crispy five-spice chicken

chinese simmered star anise pork

roast spice lamb and eggplant

2 tablespoons cumin seeds
1 tablespoon coriander seeds
2 x 6-cutlet lamb racks
3 tablespoons olive oil
2 eggplants (aubergines), thickly sliced
sea salt and cracked black pepper

Preheat the oven to 200°C (400°F). Place the cumin and coriander seeds in a dry frying pan over medium heat and toast the seeds for 2 minutes or until fragrant. Place the seeds in a spice grinder or mortar and pestle and grind into a rough powder.
Brush the lamb racks with a little of the olive oil and press half of the spice powder onto them. Place the eggplant slices in a baking dish and drizzle with the remaining olive oil. Sprinkle with sea salt and cracked black pepper, then with the remaining spice mix. Place the lamb racks on top and bake for 20 minutes or until the lamb is cooked to your liking and the eggplant is soft. Slice the racks in half and serve with the eggplant. Serves 4.

crispy five-spice chicken

4 chicken breast fillets
plain (all-purpose) flour, for coating
2 eggs, lightly beaten
oil, to shallow-fry
coating mixture
2½ teaspoons Chinese five-spice powder
2 cups fine fresh breadcrumbs
2 teaspoons ground cumin
2 teaspoons ground coriander
1 teaspoon sea salt
cracked black pepper
1 tablespoon finely chopped fresh flat-leaf parsley

Cut the chicken breast fillets in half lengthways. Dust the chicken lightly in flour and set aside.
To make the coating mixture, combine the Chinese five-spice, breadcrumbs, cumin, coriander, salt, pepper and parsley. Dip the chicken into beaten egg and then press firmly into the coating mixture. Heat 1cm (½ inch) of oil in a frying pan over medium–high heat. Add the chicken to the pan and cook for 2–3 minutes each side or until golden and crisp. Drain on absorbent paper.
Serve the chicken with steamed Asian greens. Serves 4.

chinese simmered star anise pork

1 tablespoon sesame oil*
1 tablespoon shredded ginger
1 cup Chinese cooking wine* or sherry
¼ cup (2 fl oz) soy sauce
¼ cup (2 fl oz) hoisin sauce*
2 tablespoons sugar
2 star anise
4 pork fillets, trimmed

Heat the sesame oil in a frying pan over low heat. Add the shredded ginger and cook for 1 minute, then add the cooking wine, soy sauce, hoisin sauce, sugar and star anise and allow to simmer. Add the pork to the pan and cover. Cook for 5 minutes each side or until the pork is tender.
Remove the pork from the pan and set aside. Allow the sauce to continue simmering until it has reduced and thickened. To serve, slice the pork and place in a serving bowl. Spoon over the sauce from the frying pan and serve with rice and steamed greens. Serves 4.

duck in star anise broth

1 Chinese barbecued duck*
8 cups (64 fl oz) chicken stock
2 star anise
1 cinnamon stick
4 slices ginger
200g (6½ oz) Chinese broccoli* (gai larn), halved
300g (10 oz) fresh udon noodles*
3 spring (green) onions, sliced

Cut the duck into small pieces and remove most of the bones. Place the chicken stock, star anise, cinnamon stick and ginger in a saucepan over medium heat and simmer for 5 minutes. Add the Chinese broccoli and udon noodles and cook for 4 minutes. Add the duck pieces to the broth and allow to simmer for 2 minutes or until heated through. Skim any fat from the top of the soup and remove the cinnamon stick and star anise.
To serve, ladle the soup into bowls and sprinkle with spring onions. Serves 4.
note – If Chinese barbecued duck is not available, place a couple of star anise and a cinnamon stick in the cavity of a duck or chicken, then brush with dark soy sauce and roast until tender.

duck in star anise broth

cinnamon-smoked duck

4 duck breasts
2 cinnamon sticks, roughly crumbled
2 tablespoons white rice
2 tablespoons sugar
1 star anise, lightly crushed
6 bok choy*, halved
2 tablespoons soy sauce
2 teaspoons sesame oil*

Heat a frying pan over high heat. Prick the skin of the duck firmly with a fork, then add the breasts to the pan, skin-side down, and cook for 4 minutes or until the skin is a deep golden colour. Turn the duck breasts and cook the other side for 1 minute. Set aside.
Place the cinnamon, rice, sugar and star anise in a piece of foil and turn up the edges to make a shallow cup. Place this foil cup in the base of a wok, then put a metal rack in the wok and lay the duck breasts on top of it. Cover the wok tightly with a lid and place the wok over high heat. Allow the duck breasts to smoke for 5 minutes, or longer for a more intense smoke flavour.
Steam the bok choy over boiling water and place on serving plates. Top with a duck breast and sprinkle with soy sauce and sesame oil. Serve with steamed jasmine rice. Serves 4.

moroccan-spiced veal with quinces

2 tablespoons olive oil
8 thick slices veal shank
plain (all-purpose) flour, for coating
1 tablespoon ground cumin
1 tablespoon ground coriander
1 cinnamon stick
1 tablespoon grated orange rind
2 red onions, chopped
4 cups (32 fl oz) beef stock
2 quinces, peeled, cored and quartered

Heat the oil in a large, deep frying pan over high heat. Lightly coat the veal with flour and shake off any excess. Cook in the hot pan for 3 minutes each side, or until well browned. Remove the veal from the pan and set aside. Add the cumin, coriander, cinnamon stick, orange rind and onion to the frying pan and cook, stirring occasionally, for 5 minutes. Add the beef stock, the browned veal and the quinces. Cover and simmer for 35 minutes, then turn the veal and simmer for a further 35 minutes or until the veal and quinces are tender. Serve with couscous. Serves 4. note – If quinces are unavailable, use halved, cored and peeled apples or firm pears and add them in the last 35 minutes of cooking.

spiced beef salad with hummus dressing

750g (1½ lb) rump or fillet steak
2 teaspoons ground cumin
1 tablespoon harissa* (chilli paste)
2 tablespoons lemon juice
2 cloves garlic, crushed
4 thick slices bread, toasted
150g (5 oz) salad greens
hummus dressing
½ cup cooked chick peas
3 tablespoons lemon juice
3 tablespoons olive oil
2 tablespoons tahini*
1 teaspoon ground cumin
3–4 tablespoons water

Trim the steak of fat and place in a shallow dish with the combined cumin, harissa, lemon juice and garlic. Refrigerate for 30 minutes to marinate.
While the steak is marinating, make the hummus dressing by placing the chick peas, lemon juice, olive oil, tahini and cumin in a food processor and processing until finely chopped. Add enough water to make a smooth dressing. Grill or barbecue the steak until cooked to your liking. Slice the steak. Place the toasted bread and salad on serving plates. Top with the steak and hummus dressing and serve with lemon wedges. Serves 4.

coconut fish curry

1 tablespoon peanut oil
2 teaspoons ground cumin
2 teaspoons ground coriander
2 green chillies, sliced
1 cinnamon stick
1 star anise
6 kaffir lime leaves, lightly crushed
3½ cups (28 fl oz) coconut cream
4 x 180g (6 oz) firm white fish fillets, halved
4 tablespoons lime juice
fresh coriander (cilantro) leaves, to serve

Heat the oil in a large frying pan over medium heat. Add the cumin, ground coriander, chillies, cinnamon stick, star anise and kaffir lime leaves and cook, stirring, for 2 minutes or until fragrant. Add the coconut cream and reduce the heat. Allow to simmer for 5 minutes.
Add the fish to the coconut curry sauce and simmer for 4 minutes each side or until the fish is tender. Remove the cinnamon, star anise and lime leaves from the sauce, then stir through the lime juice. To serve, place the fish and curry sauce in serving bowls and top with coriander leaves. Serve with steamed rice. Serves 4.

cinnamon-smoked duck

spiced beef salad with hummus dressing

moroccan-spiced veal with quinces

coconut fish curry

burnt honey and star anise creams

cinnamon jelly with plums

cinnamon apple sour cream cake

burnt honey and star anise creams

1 cup (8 fl oz) milk
1 cup (8 fl oz) cream
3 star anise
1 cinnamon stick
1/3 cup caster (superfine) sugar
3 eggs
1/3 cup (2¾ fl oz) honey

Preheat the oven to 160°C (315°F). Place the milk, cream, star anise and cinnamon stick in a saucepan over low heat and heat until hot but not boiling. Reduce the heat and allow to simmer for 3 minutes, then remove from the heat and leave to infuse for 10 minutes.

Remove the star anise and cinnamon from the saucepan. Whisk together the sugar and eggs. Stir in the slightly cooled milk mixture and pour into six ½-cup (4 fl oz) capacity ovenproof bowls or glasses. Place in a baking tray filled with enough hot water to come halfway up the sides of the bowls or glasses. Bake for 25 minutes or until the creams are only just set, then remove from the baking dish and refrigerate for 2 hours or until cool.

Top each cream with 2 teaspoons of honey. Place under a hot grill until the honey is a deep golden colour. Leave for 3 minutes before serving. Serves 6.

cinnamon jelly with plums

3 cinnamon sticks
1 cup (8 fl oz) sweet dessert wine
1 cup (8 fl oz) water
1/3 cup sugar
1 tablespoon gelatine
1/4 cup (2 fl oz) water, extra
4 plums, halved, sprinkled with sugar and grilled

Place the cinnamon sticks, wine, water and sugar in a saucepan over medium heat and simmer for 5 minutes. Remove the cinnamon sticks.

Place the gelatine in a bowl and pour over the extra water. Allow to stand for 5 minutes. Pour the gelatine mixture into the cinnamon syrup and return to the heat. Bring the mixture to the boil and boil for 2 minutes to completely dissolve the gelatine.

Pour the mixture into four lightly oiled ½-cup (4 fl oz) capacity moulds or ramekins and place in the refrigerator for 2–3 hours or until set. To serve, unmould the jellies onto serving plates. Serve with halved plums. Serves 4.

cinnamon apple sour cream cake

125g (4 oz) butter
2/3 cup caster (superfine) sugar
2 teaspoons ground cinnamon
2 eggs
2/3 cup (5½ fl oz) sour cream
1½ cups self-raising (self-rising) flour
topping
3 tablespoons plain (all-purpose) flour
3 tablespoons demerara sugar*
3 tablespoons almond meal (ground almonds)
1 teaspoon ground cinnamon
2 green apples, peeled, cored and thinly sliced

Preheat the oven to 180°C (350°F). Place the butter, sugar and cinnamon in the bowl of an electric mixer and beat until light and creamy. Add the eggs and beat well. Fold the sour cream through the mixture and then sift the flour over. Fold through until combined. Spoon the cake mixture into a greased 23cm (9 inch) round springform pan. To make the topping, mix together the flour, demerara sugar, almonds and cinnamon and toss the apples in the mixture. Arrange the apples on top of the cake and sprinkle with any remaining topping. Bake for 1 hour or until the cake is cooked when tested with a skewer. Serve warm or cool in wedges with thick cream. Serves 8.

cinnamon and mascarpone ice cream

1½ cups sugar
1¾ cups (14 fl oz) water
2 teaspoons ground cinnamon
450g (14 oz) mascarpone*
1/2 cup (4 fl oz) cream

Place the sugar and water in a saucepan over low heat and stir until the sugar has dissolved. Simmer for 3 minutes, then remove from the heat, add the cinnamon and leave the syrup until cool.

Mix the syrup with the mascarpone and cream. Place in an ice cream maker and follow the manufacturer's instructions until the ice cream is thick and scoopable. Alternatively, place the mixture in a metal container and freeze, beating well at 1-hour intervals, until the ice cream is scoopable. Serve in scoops with fruit and crisp biscuits. Serves 6.

note – If mascarpone is not available, combine equal quantities of cream cheese and thick (double) cream.

cinnamon and mascarpone ice cream

glossary

arborio rice

Taking its name from a village in the Piedmont region of northern Italy, this short-grain rice is used for risotto, a dish of rice cooked in stock. The grains of rice release some of their starch when cooked, giving the dish a creamy texture. Other rice varieties used for risotto include vialone and carnaroli.

bamboo steamer

This woven Asian bamboo container has a lid and slatted base. Placed on top of a saucepan of boiling water, the steamer contains the food—meats, vegetables or noodles—to be steamed. These inexpensive steamers are available from Asian food stores and most cook shops.

beef stock

See stock

black sesame seeds

The seeds of an annual herb, black sesame seeds are largely used in Japanese cookery. The raw seeds have an earthy taste and should not be toasted, otherwise they become bitter. Black sesame seeds come from the same family as white sesame seeds. Substitute white sesame seeds if black seeds are not available.

blanching

A cooking method in which foods are plunged into boiling unsalted water for a few seconds or minutes, removed and then refreshed under cold water to stop the cooking process. Blanching is used to slightly soften the texture, heighten the colour and enhance the flavour of foods. Vegetables can also be blanched before freezing to destroy the enzymes that cause them to perish.

bok choy

Also called Chinese chard or Chinese white cabbage, this mildly flavoured green should only be cooked for a few minutes in order to retain colour and texture. Baby bok choy can be cooked whole. The larger type should be washed well and the leaves separated. Trim off the dark green leaf, leaving only the narrow border along the white leaf rib.

capers

These are the green flower buds from a Mediterranean shrub. The buds are picked before they open and are preserved in a brine solution or in salt. I prefer to use the salted capers because of their firm texture. Rinse away the salt before using them. Available from good delicatessens.

chervil

This delicate, lacy-looking herb has a faint, sweet aniseed flavour. Its flavour diminishes after chopping, so add to food just before serving. Choose leaves that are a clear green.

chicken stock

See stock

chinese barbecued duck

Cooked ducks, spiced and barbecued in the traditional Chinese style, are avaliable from Chinese barbecue shops or Chinese food stores.

chinese barbecued pork

Cooked pork meat, spiced and barbecued in the traditional Chinese barbecue style, is avaliable from Chinese barbecue shops or Chinese food stores.

chinese broccoli

Also called gai larn or Chinese kale, this leafy vegetable has dark green leaves, stout stems and small white flowers. The stem is the main part of the plant eaten. Wash thoroughly, then peel and split the tough stems before steaming, boiling, braising or stir-frying.

chinese cooking wine

This wine, blended from glutinous rice, millet, a special yeast and local spring waters, comes from the town of Shao hsing in northern China. Chinese cooking wine is similar to dry sherry and is mostly used in Asian cooking to braise foods. It can be found in Asian supermarkets, usually labelled as shao hsing.

chocolate

melting

The golden rule when melting chocolate is not to cook it. There are a few ways to melt chocolate. The best is to melt it over hot water. This is done by placing the chocolate in a heat-resistant bowl or in the top of a double boiler over a saucepan of simmering water. Make sure the base of the bowl containing the chocolate is not touching the water, as this can cause the chocolate to burn. Be sure also that no steam or water comes into contact with the chocolate, as this causes the chocolate to seize into a hard lump which cannot be remelted. Allow the chocolate to melt slowly while stirring it constantly. Chocolate can be melted over direct heat when it has been combined with other ingredients like butter or cream. The heat should be low and the mixture should be stirred constantly during the melting process.

tempering

Dark and semi-sweet chocolates are high in cocoa butter and cocoa liquor and therefore need to go through the tempering process to ensure the chocolate sets and has a shiny finish. This is necessary when making chocolate moulds or spreads. To temper, melt the chocolate as above. Stir the chocolate until it reaches a temperature of 45°C (113°F). Use a sugar thermometer to measure the temperature. Remove the bowl from the heat and sit it in a dish of cold water. Stir the chocolate until it begins to set around the edges. Return the bowl to the heat and stir until the chocolate melts again and reaches a temperature of 32°C (90°F). The chocolate is now tempered.

couscous

Having the appearance of rough sand, this grain product from northern Africa is as versatile as rice or pasta but has a much more earthy and nutty flavour. Made by grinding whole grains and rubbing them by hand with a little salted water into small balls, couscous is best prepared by soaking in hot stock or steaming over a simmering, flavourful stew. Separate the grains with a fork and toss with butter before serving.

crème fraîche

A mixture of naturally soured cream and fresh cream, crème fraîche is lighter and not as thick as the easily obtainable sour cream, although sour cream does make a good substitute for crème fraîche. Available from gourmet food stores and some large supermarkets.

dariole moulds

See tins and moulds

demerara sugar

This sugar was originally made in Demerara, Guyana. The small, hard crystals are made by adding a little molasses to white sugar, giving the sugar a distinct caramel-like flavour and sticky texture. If unavailable, use ¾ white sugar and ¼ brown.

du puy lentils

The king of lentils, these very small, dark-green legumes, grown in the Auvergne at Le Puy, have a great texture and a wonderful earthy and nutty flavour. These lentils are imported from France and can be expensive. Available from gourmet food stores or health food stores.

feta (marinated)

This firm cheese was traditionally made using sheeps' milk or a combination of sheeps' and goats' milk. Today, feta is made from cows' milk. The firm blocks of cheese are matured in a salty whey. The feta is usually sold this way, or marinated in an oil flavoured with herbs, peppercorns or chillies. I like to purchase a creamy feta with its flavoured oil, as the feta has a wonderful flavour and the oil can be used along with the cheese as part of a dressing for a salad or pasta.

fish sauce

This clear, amber-tinted liquid is drained from salted, fermented fish. A very important flavouring in Thai cuisine, it is available from supermarkets and Asian food stores.

fish stock

See stock

gai larn

See Chinese broccoli

gravlax

Resembling smoked salmon but with a more delicate flavour, this Nordic speciality consists of a salmon fillet cured in a combination of rock salt, sugar and herbs. Available from delicatessens and some supermarkets.

harissa

This hot paste of red chillies, garlic, spices and olive oil is available in tubes or jars from delicatessens.

hoisin sauce

A thick, sweet-tasting Chinese sauce, made from fermented soy beans, sugar, salt and red rice and used as a dipping sauce or glaze. Traditionally used for Peking duck, it is available from Asian food stores.

japanese pumpkin

This variety of pumpkin has a thin, green and white, almost striped skin with a moist and bright-orange sweet flesh. The thin skin and soft flesh of this pumpkin make it easy to peel and cut. The sweetness of the pumpkin intensifies with cooking.

kecap manis

This very thick, sweet but salty soy sauce originated in Java, Indonesia, where it is still used as a flavouring or condiment not unlike soy sauce. Available from Asian food stores.

laksa paste

The base to an Asian coconut milk soup, laksa paste can contain ground spices, herbs, ginger, shrimp paste and lemongrass. The soup contains a spiced coconut broth, noodles, vegetables such as bean sprouts, mint and coriander, and seafood or chicken. Available from supermarkets or Asian food stores.

lemongrass

A tall, lemon-scented grass used in Asian, mainly Thai, cooking. Peel away outer leaves and use the tender root end of the grass. Chop finely or use in pieces to infuse flavour (remove the pieces from the dish before serving). Available from Asian food stores, good fruit and vegetable shops and most supermarkets.

linguini

A long, thin pasta with square-cut edges, linguini is similar to flat spaghetti. Spaghetti or fettuccine makes a suitable substitute.

mascarpone

An Italian triple-cream curd-style fresh cheese, which has a similar consistency to double or thick cream. Available from good delicatessens and some supermarkets.

melting chocolate

See chocolate

mortar and pestle

This essential kitchen tool consists of a deep-sided bowl and a rounded, club-shaped implement used for crushing or pulverising wet or dry ingredients, including spices, herbs and garlic.

non-reactive bowl

A ceramic or glass bowl, often necessary when high concentrations of vinegar or acidic foods are used.

non-reactive saucepan

Often necessary when high concentrations of vinegar or acidic foods are used. Use any saucepan except those that are made from aluminium.

noodles

egg noodles

Whether fresh or dry, these noodles come in a variety of thicknesses and shapes. Great for soups or stir-fries, dry egg noodles need to be cooked in rapidly boiling water before being added to a recipe. Fresh noodles need only be rinsed or plunged into boiling water. Available from Asian food stores and supermarkets.

fresh rice noodles

These come in a variety of widths and lengths and are located in the refrigerator section of Asian food stores and some supermarkets. Keep them only for a few days in the refrigerator. To prepare, soak the noodles in hot to boiling water for 1 minute, separating them gently with a fork, then drain. Fresh rice noodles also come as rolls. These can be steamed as a side dish or filled and steamed.

somen noodles

These are fine, white Japanese noodles made from wheat flour mixed with water or egg yolk, and occasionally flavoured with green tea. Somen noodles are often sold tied in bundles in their packets. Available from Japanese food stores and some Asian supermarkets.

rice noodle rolls

These are thick, fresh rice noodles that have been rolled into a sausage-like shape. Purchased from Asian food stores, these rolls are available plain or sometimes stuffed with prawns and herbs. They are easily prepared by steaming over boiling water until soft. Because these noodle rolls are bought fresh, they will only keep for 5–7 days.

rice paper wrappers or rounds

These are transparent, circular wrappers made from a paste of ground rice and water. Before using, brush or dip in warm water until they are pliable. These rice paper wrappers should not be confused with the thick white rice sheets used for making sweets such as nougat. Rice paper wrappers are available from Asian food stores and come in a range of sizes.

rice-stick noodles

This is a general name given to dry rice noodles that are of a similar thickness to fettuccine. Rice-stick noodles are the noodles used in the classic dish Phad Thai. They are also commonly used in Vietnam. The noodles need to be soaked in boiling water to rehydrate them before adding to stir-fries or soups.

rice vermicelli noodles

These very fine, ready-cooked noodles are most often used in soups such as laksa. Rice vermicelli noodles are easy to prepare. Simply soak them in boiling water to loosen up the strands, then drain before combining with other ingredients.

udon noodles

These white Japanese wheat noodles can be purchased from Japanese or Asian food stores either fresh in vacuum packs (look in the refrigerator section), or dried. They come in a variety of thicknesses and lengths and are either flat or round. Udon noodles are most commonly used in Japanese soups.

ovenproof dishes

See tins and moulds

palm sugar

This is the sap of several varieties of palm tree concentrated into a heavy, moist sugar. Used mainly in Thai cooking, it is sold in block form and should be grated or shaved before using. I prefer the darker one for its stronger caramel flavour. Substitue brown sugar if palm sugar is not available.

pancetta

Italian rolled and cured meat similar to prosciutto only not as salty or as tough. Can be eaten in thin slices from the roll or cooked in dishes.

pasta

3 cups flour
4 large eggs
2 teaspoons salt

Place the flour on a bench top in a mound. Make a hole in the mound and break the eggs into it, also adding the salt. Break up the eggs with a fork and gradually add flour to the eggs until a rough dough forms. (You can do this step in a food processor.) Place the dough on a lightly floured surface (you may need to add a little flour to make the dough manageable) and knead until it is smooth. Cut the pasta into four pieces and roll through a pasta machine, or use a rolling pin, until it is the desired thickness. Cut the pasta into shapes or cover with a damp cloth if you are using it a few hours later. Cook the pasta in plenty of boiling water until it is al dente. Make sure the water stays boiling while the pasta cooks. To dry, hang the pasta over a suspended wooden spoon or a clean broom handle for 1–2 hours, or until it is dry and hard. Store pasta in airtight containers.

pastry

shortcrust pastry

2 cups plain (all-purpose) flour
155g (5 oz) butter, chopped
iced water

Place the flour and butter in a food processor and process until the mixture has formed fine crumbs. Add enough iced water to form a soft dough. Remove the dough from the food processor and knead lightly. Wrap the dough in plastic wrap and refrigerate for 30 minutes before rolling to prevent shrinkage when baked. Makes 1 quantity.

sweet shortcrust pastry

2 cups plain (all-purpose) flour
3 tablespoons caster (superfine) sugar
155g (5 oz) butter, chopped
iced water

Place the flour, sugar and butter in a food processor and process until the mixture has formed fine crumbs. Add enough iced water to form a soft dough. Remove the dough from the food processor and knead lightly. Wrap the dough in plastic wrap and refrigerate for 30 minutes before rolling to prevent shrinkage when baked. Makes 1 quantity.

prosciutto

A type of Italian ham which has been salted and then air dried for between 8 months and 2 years. Sold in paper-thin slices for eating raw or for using in cooked dishes.

ramekins

See tins and moulds

removable-base tart tins

See tins and moulds

rosewater

This is the extracted fragrance of roses, made by distilling rose petals in water. Rosewater is used throughout the Indian subcontinent and the Middle East for desserts, sweets and beverages. Available from health food stores and delicatessens.

saffron threads

The dried stigma of the crocus flower, saffron is an aromatic, highly-prized spice consisting of a mass of orange-red threadlike strands. Use as a flavouring for both sweet and savoury dishes, and make sure you buy true saffron in strands, not powdered imitations which are usually made of turmeric.

sashimi

Finest quality fish cut in an Asian or Japanese style, this is very tender and is used raw in Japanese cuisine. Often used sparingly due to price. Available from good fish markets.

sesame oil

An important cooking oil in many Asian cuisines, being free of unwanted odours and having good keeping qualities. It is high in poly-unsaturated fatty acids and has a fragrant, nutty flavour.

shortcrust pastry

See pastry

spice grinder

Used to grind whole spices to a fine or coarse powder. Some are manual —that is, they have handles you have to turn—and others are electric, doubling as coffee grinders. If using the electric type, clean well after each use so you don't get spices in your coffee, and vice versa.

sponge cake

4 eggs

½ cup caster (superfine) sugar

½ cup plain (all-purpose) flour

60g (2 oz) butter, melted and cooled

1 teaspoon vanilla extract

Preheat the oven to 160°C (315°F). Place the eggs and sugar in the bowl of an electric mixer and beat for 10 minutes or until the mixture is thick and pale. Sift the flour over the egg mixture and gently fold through. Add the butter and vanilla to the mixture and carefully fold to combine. Pour the mixture into a 23cm (9 inch) round cake tin that has been greased and base-lined with baking paper and bake for 35–40 minutes. Cool in the tin for 20 minutes, then turn onto a wire rack to cool completely.

springform pans

See tins and moulds

sterilised jars

Before putting foods into jars to be sealed and stored, the jars need to be sterilised. Sterilise the jars by thoroughly washing in hot water, but don't dry with a tea towel. Place the jars on a baking tray in a preheated 100°C (200°F) oven for 30 minutes. Remove the jars from the oven, allow to cool, then fill as the recipe requires and seal.

stock

beef stock

1½ kg (3 lb) beef bones, cut into pieces

2 onions, quartered

2 carrots, quartered

2 stalks celery, cut into large pieces

assorted fresh herbs

2 bay leaves

10 peppercorns

4 litres (16 cups or 128 fl oz) water

Preheat the oven to 220°C (425°F). Place the bones on a baking tray and bake for 30 minutes. Add the onions and carrots and bake for a further 20 minutes. Transfer the bones, onions and carrots to a stock pot or large saucepan. Skim the fat from the juices in the baking tray, then add 2 cups (8 fl oz) of boiling water to the tray and pour the juices into the saucepan. Add the celery, herbs, bay leaves, peppercorns and water and bring to the boil. Simmer for 4–5 hours or until the stock has a good flavour. Skim the surface as the stock simmers, then strain and use as the recipe requires. Refrigerate the beef stock for up to 3 days or freeze for up to 3 months. Makes 2½–3 litres (10–12 cups or 80–96 fl oz).

chicken stock

1½ kg (3 lb) chicken bones, cut into pieces

2 onions, quartered

2 carrots, quartered

2 stalks celery, cut into large pieces

assorted fresh herbs

2 bay leaves

10 peppercorns

4 litres (16 cups or 128 fl oz) water

Place all the ingredients in a stock pot or large saucepan and simmer for 3–4 hours or until the stock is well flavoured. Skim the surface as the stock simmers, then strain and use as the recipe requires. Refrigerate the chicken stock for up to 3 days or freeze for up to 3 months. Makes 2½–3 litres (10–12 cups or 80–96 fl oz). For a brown chicken stock, brush the chicken bones with a little oil and roast in a baking dish for 30 minutes before making the stock.

fish stock

1 tablespoon butter

1 onion, finely chopped

750g (1½ lb) fish bones, chopped

1 cup (8 fl oz) white wine

1 litre (4 cups or 32 fl oz) water

10 peppercorns

3–4 sprigs mild herbs

1 bay leaf

Place the butter and onion in a large saucepan over low heat and cook for 10 minutes or until the onion is soft but not browned. Add the fish bones, wine, water, peppercorns, herbs and bay leaf and simmer for 20 minutes. Skim the surface as the stock simmers, then strain and use as the recipe requires. Refrigerate the fish stock for up to 2 days or freeze for up to 2 months. Makes 3–3½ cups (24–28 fl oz). *Note*: do not simmer stock for more than 20 minutes or it will sour.

vegetable stock

4 litres (16 cups or 128 fl oz) water

1 parsnip, chopped

2 onions, quartered

1 clove garlic, peeled

2 carrots, quartered

300g (10 oz) cabbage, roughly chopped

3 stalks celery, cut into large pieces

assorted fresh herbs

2 bay leaves

1 tablespoon peppercorns

Place all the ingredients in a stock pot or large saucepan and allow to simmer for 2 hours or until the stock has a good flavour. Skim the surface as the stock simmers, then strain and use as the recipe requires. Refrigerate vegetable stock for up to 4 days or freeze for up to 8 months. Makes 2½–3 litres (10–12 cups or 80–96 fl oz).

sweet shortcrust pastry
See pastry

tahini
A thick, smooth and oily paste made from lightly toasted and ground sesame seeds. Available in jars from most supermarkets, it is often used in savoury dips.

tempering
See chocolate

tins and moulds
dariole moulds
These are small cylindrical metal or plastic moulds with slightly sloping sides, used to make puddings or for set desserts, such as mousses, jellies and crème caramels.

ovenproof dishes
These dishes of various shapes and sizes are usually made from glazed ceramic. Check the labels before purchasing to be sure that the dish is ovenproof. Most ovenproof dishes can also be transferred directly from the freezer to the oven.

ramekins
Small, ovenproof dishes used for soufflés, crème brûlées and other individually served foods. Ramekins are usually made from porcelain and have roughened bases to help them stick to the base of a roasting tin when baking in a boiling water bath.

removable-base tart tins
Metal tins with fluted sides that double the surface area exposed to the heat, helping pastry crusts to cook more quickly. The bases are removable to aid in unmoulding the tarts or pies.

springform pans
These are used for fragile or soft-topped cakes like cheesecakes, enabling them to be unmoulded without the need for inverting the pan. Simply unbuckle the clip at the side of the pan and lift it off the base.

vanilla sugar
2 vanilla beans
1 cup caster (superfine) sugar

Finely chop the vanilla beans and place in a food processor with the sugar. Process until the vanilla is very finely chopped through the sugar. You may like to press the sugar through a sieve to remove any large pieces of the vanilla bean that remain. Store the vanilla sugar in an airtight container and use in baking or wherever a mellow sweet vanilla taste is required. Makes 1 cup.

vegetable stock
See stock

verjuice
Made from the sour juice of unripe grapes or crabapples, this acidic liquid, which literally means 'green juice', is used where a piquant, vinegar-like flavour is required. Verjuice can be made by extracting the juice from unripe green grapes, or can be purchased in bottles from good delicatessens.

wasabi paste
A pungent condiment made from the knobbly green root of the Japanese plant *Wasabia japonica*. Traditionally served with Japanese sushi and sashimi, it causes the same warming and nasal-stinging sensation as horseradish. Available from Asian food stores.

conversion chart

1 teaspoon = 5ml
1 Australian tablespoon = 20ml (4 teaspoons)
1 UK tablespoon = 15ml (3 teaspoons or ½ fl oz)
1 cup = 250ml (8 fl oz)

cup conversions

1 cup baby English spinach, firmly packed = 60g (2 oz)
1 cup basil leaves, whole, firmly packed = 50g (1¾ oz)
1 cup cheese, parmesan, finely grated = 100g (3½ oz)
1 cup coriander (cilantro) leaves, whole = 30g (1 oz)
1 cup couscous = 200g (6½ oz)
1 cup flour, white = 125g (4 oz)
1 cup lentils = 200g (6½ oz)
1 cup parsley, flat-leaf (Italian), whole = 20g (¾ oz)
1 cup rice, uncooked = 220g (7 oz)
1 cup rocket (arugula) leaves, roughly chopped = 45g (1½ oz)
1 cup sour cream = 250g (8 oz)
1 cup sugar, caster (superfine) and demerara = 220g (7 oz)
1 cup sugar, white = 250g (8 oz)
1 cup yoghurt, plain = 250g (8 oz)

liquid conversions

metric	imperial	US cups
30 ml	1 fl oz	⅛ cup
60 ml	2 fl oz	¼ cup
80 ml	2¾ fl oz	⅓ cup
125 ml	4 fl oz	½ cup
185 ml	6 fl oz	¾ cup
250 ml	8 fl oz	1 cup
375 ml	12 fl oz	1½ cups
500 ml	16 fl oz	2 cups
600 ml	20 fl oz	2½ cups
750 ml	24 fl oz	3 cups
1 litre	32 fl oz	4 cups

index